Better Homes and Gardens®

CanIt!

WILEY

JOHN WILEY & SONS, INC.

Library of Congress Cataloging-in-Publication Data is available upon request.

ISBN 978-1-118-21718-4(pbk); ISBN 978-1-118-21719-1(ebk);

ISBN 978-1-118-21720-7(ebk); ISBN 978-1-118-21721-4(ebk)

Printed in the United States of America

10 9 8 7 6 5 4 3 2 1

Meredith Corporation

Editor: Jan Miller

Contributing Editor: Lisa Kingsley, Waterbury Publications, Inc.

Contributing Photographer: Scott Little

Contributing Food Stylist: Sue Hoss, Main Dish Media

John Wiley & Sons, Inc.

Publisher: Natalie Chapman

Associate Publisher: Jessica Goodman

Executive Editor: Anne Ficklen

Editorial Assistant: Heather Dabah

Production Director: Diana Cisek

Senior Production Editor: Amy Zarkos

Manufacturing Manager: Tom Hyland

Design Director: Ken Carlson, Waterbury Publications, Inc.

Associate Design Director: Bruce Yang, Waterbury Publications, Inc.

Production Assistant: Mindy Samuelson, Waterbury Publications, Inc.

Our seal assures you that every recipe in *Can It!* has been tested in the Better Homes and Gardens® Test Kitchen. This means that each recipe is practical and reliable and meets our high standards of taste appeal. We guarantee your satisfaction with this book for as long as you own it.

table of contents

SUMMER IN A JAR

WHETHER YOU GROW YOUR OWN fruits and vegetables, are a dedicated patron of your local farmer's market, or simply want to capture the best peak-season produce at the lowest prices in the supermarket, there are so many good reasons to can your own food.

FLAVOR. Few things taste better on a cold fall or winter night than a bowl of pasta tossed with tomato sauce simmered from fat, juicy, sweet, and deeply red August tomatoes. Few things brighten the beginning of a gray day in March more than toast slathered with jewel-tone jam made in July from perfectly ripe raspberries. *Taste a little of the summer*, writes Greg Brown in his song "Canned Goods," extolling the pleasures of eating food that has been put up at its peak. *My grandma's put it all in jars.*

HEALTHFULNESS. When you can your own food, you control virtually every aspect of what goes into it. Fruits and vegetables are naturally healthful, but you can protect their nutritional integrity and tailor your home-canned products to suit your taste and lifestyle. They can be all-natural or organic, with minimal sugar, salt, or fat, and no preservatives.

ECONOMY. Canning your own food is a great way to save money on the grocery bills—especially if you grow your own produce. After the initial outlay for equipment, each gorgeous jar of food costs just pennies. Great abundance is created with very little in terms of dollars.

EMOTIONAL SATISFACTION. Rows of gleaming, colorful jars of home-canned food on a pantry shelf are good for both body and soul. Not only do you know there are months of good eating at your fingertips, but it is also deeply rewarding to put up your own food. Canning allows you to move through the year with the rhythm of the seasons—a truly healthful way to live.

Whether you are an experienced canner or have never so much as snapped a bean, *Better Homes and Gardens® Can It!* provides all the information and inspiration you need to stock your pantry with home-canned food. *Can It!* offers the safest, simplest, and most up-to-date methods to ensure success, and there is something for every taste and occasion. Recipes include classic favorites such as Strawberry Jam and Best-Ever Dill Pickles to more exotic offerings such as Blood Orange and Beaujolais Marmalade and Fire-Roasted Tomato-Ancho Taco Sauce.

Get the water boiling and get canning!

Summer in a Jar

Can It!

CHAPTER 1

Canning Basics

Here's everything you need to know to get started canning—the types of methods, ingredients, equipment—and exactly how to keep your food delicious and safe to eat.

THE FIVE RULES OF CANNING

Follow these basic rules exactly to ensure food safety and success.

1 KNOW WHICH CANNER TO USE The boiling-water canner—basically a big pot with a lid and a rack in the bottom—is used for high-acid foods, which naturally resist bacteria growth. Pressure canners are used with low-acid foods and recipes that are especially prone to harboring harmful microorganisms. They heat food hotter than boiling-water canners.

The recipe will specify which type of canner is appropriate. In this book, all of the recipes use a boiling-water canner. (See pages 20–21 for more information.)

2 CHOOSE THE RIGHT JARS Use jars made specifically for canning. Don't use glass jars from purchased food, even if they look like canning jars. Don't use jars that look different from the canning jars currently on the market. And avoid jars with chipped edges because that can affect the seal.

Use the size jar specified in the recipe. (See page 12 for more information.)

3 USE LIDS PROPERLY Use the special two-piece lids manufactured for canning.

Reuse rings, but do not reuse lids, which have a sticky compound that seals the jar.

Don't screw lids on too tightly or they won't create a vacuum seal properly. Heat the lids in very hot but not boiling water or the compound won't seal. Test for sealing on each jar after it has cooled. (See page 21 for more information.)

4 CHOOSE THE RIGHT RECIPE Modern canning recipes are safer than those from just 20 years ago. Foods may be processed longer or hotter. Always use tested recipes from reliable, current sources—and follow the recipes exactly. Don't alter ingredients. Alterations can compromise food safety. (See page 17 for more information.)

5 KEEP IT CLEAN AND KEEP IT HOT Keep everything scrupulously clean. Wash and sterilize jars. Pack hot food into hot jars one at a time—not assembly-line style. Take only one jar out of the canner at a time and as soon as it's filled, place it back in the simmering water in the canner. (See pages 20–21 for more information.)

BOILING-WATER CANNER

A boiling-water canner heats jars to 212°F, enough to kill microorganisms found in high-acid foods (see page 11). The rack allows water to flow beneath the jars for even heating. It also has handles that allow you to lower and lift jars easily into the hot water. Canners come in different sizes and finishes. A traditional speckled enamel finish resists chips and rust well. High-end boiling-water canners are available in sleek polished steel.

HIGH-ACID AND LOW-ACID FOODS

In canning, the acidity level of foods is critical. High-acid foods are naturally less likely to harbor harmful microorganisms, while low-acid foods require either more acid or more heat for safe canning.

Foods for canning are basically divided into two groups: low-acid and high-acid.

HIGH-ACID FOODS These are the simplest to process. Their high acidity levels create a difficult environment for microorganisms and enzymes to thrive, so processing them in the lower heat of a boiling-water canner is safe.

High-acid foods have a pH of 4.6 or lower. Lemon juice, lime juice, and vinegar are very acidic. For that reason, most pickles and most salsas are high-acid, even though they may contain foods that are otherwise low-acid, such as green beans and carrots.

LOW-ACID FOODS These foods have a pH greater than 4.6. Most vegetables are low-acid, as are most soups, stews, and meat sauces. Unless large amounts of an acidic ingredient (such as vinegar) are added, these low-acid foods must be processed in the higher heat of a pressure canner.

ACIDITY BOOSTERS Adding highly acidic elements such as lemon juice and vinegar to low-acid foods greatly broadens the types of foods you can process in a boiling-water canner because they control bacteria that can't thrive in acidic environments.

That's why canning recipes for tomatoes, which have a fairly neutral pH, often call for adding of a teaspoon of lemon juice.

It's also why green beans in a vinegary brine can be processed in a boiling-water canner (which doesn't get as hot and doesn't kill microorganisms as effectively as a pressure canner). Plain green beans, on the other hand, must be processed in the higher heat of a pressure canner.

PROCESS IN BOILING-WATER CANNER

PH LEVEL	FOOD
1.0 to 1.9	Limes
2.0 to 2.9	Lemons, strawberries
3.0 to 3.9	Gooseberries, rhubarb, pickles, oranges, peaches, sauerkraut, apples, apricots, cherries, plums, blueberries, raspberries, blackberries, pears
4.0 to 4.6	Grapes, most tomato recipes

PROCESS IN PRESSURE CANNER

PH LEVEL	FOOD
4.7 to 4.9	Plain green beans, eggplant, some tomato recipes
5.0 to 5.9	Asparagus, carrots, pumpkin, sweet peppers, beets, turnips, sweet potatoes, cucumbers, onions, cauliflower, cabbage, okra, zucchini
6.0 to 7.0	Peas, lima beans, corn, spinach

UNDERSTANDING JARS

Wide-mouth or regular-mouth? Quart or pint? There are many different types of canning jars available, each with its advantages and disadvantages. Choose the right jar for the recipe.

Home canners have a wide selection of jars from which to choose for food preservation.

Larger jars come as either wide-mouth or regular-mouth. Wide-mouth jars are ideal for packing large pieces, such as whole peaches, into a jar. Regular-mouth jars are fine for recipes such as soups and sauces.

Recipes often specify jar size. The following jars are the most widely available for home canners:

Avoid vintage jars

Old canning jars with colored glass or spring-type lids are pretty collector pieces, but they shouldn't be used in modern canning. They have irregular sizes, may crack, and don't seal properly. For refrigerator-pickled foods that don't require heat processing, decorative glass jars work fine. Just make sure you sterilize them in almost-boiling water before filling.

8-OUNCE JELLY JARS Usually with a quilted or other pattern on the side, these jars have straight sides for better freezing (no shoulders for freezing food to push up and break) and for getting every last bit of jam out of the jar.

PLASTIC FREEZER JARS Freezer jam stores well in plastic freezer containers and glass jars, but these plastic jars are just the right size, with no danger of cracking in the freezer.

QUART JARS Use these jars for any large food, such as whole tomatoes, or for a generous amount of a recipe, such as spaghetti sauce or soup for a crowd.

PINT JARS The most versatile jar, this can hold nearly anything—smaller amounts of sauce, vegetables to serve a few people, and larger amounts of jam.

4-OUNCE JARS Home-canned food doesn't last as long in the refrigerator as commercial products because no artificial preservatives are added. These small jars hold amounts you'll use up more quickly.

CANNING TOOLBOX: THE BASICS

Most of what you need to can you already have in your kitchen (see "Everyday Kitchen Tools," page 14), but a few specialty canning tools—such as a handy magnet to fish lids out of boiling water with ease—make the job much easier.

CANNING-SPECIFIC TOOLS

These few special tools make canning simpler and more efficient.

1 JAR LIFTER This tool lifts jars firmly and securely in and out of hot water. Use two hands and squeeze firmly. You can use kitchen tongs, but they are not as secure.

2 COMBINATION RULER/SPATULA The notched end is calibrated to match the most common headspaces in jars (see page 18).

The tool is also somewhat flexible with a tapered end, making it the ideal tool for slipping in along the side of filled jars to release air bubbles (see page 20).

3 MAGNETIC WAND This magic wand enables you to drop lids and rings into the hot water of the canner (no need to heat them in a separate pan) to sterilize and soften them and then easily lift them out from among jars and racks.

4 JAR FUNNELS Much wider and shorter than other funnels, these come in both wide-mouth and regular-mouth versions. They're invaluable for preventing spills when filling jars.

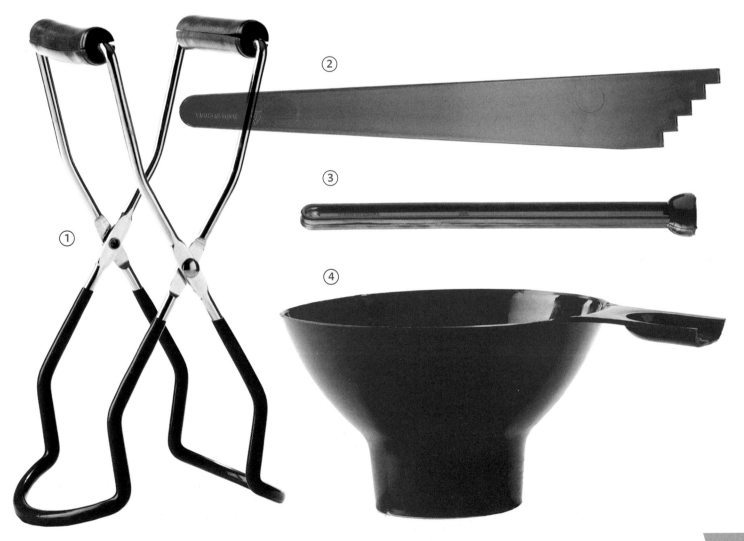

EVERYDAY KITCHEN TOOLS

Most of the tools you need for boiling-water canning are the same ones you use when you do any kind of basic cooking or baking—tools for measuring, stirring, straining, scooping, and timing.

These basic kitchen tools are necessary for successful canning.

1 8-CUP LIQUID MEASURING JAR Essential for measuring large amounts of chopped or sliced produce and for measuring large amounts of water and other liquids. It also makes a handy mixing bowl.

2 LARGE SIEVE Use this like a small colander. Rinse off small amounts of berries or set over a bowl to strain bits from liquids. Or line with cheesecloth to finely strain small amounts of liquid.

3 KITCHEN TOWELS These have many uses when canning besides drying wet utensils. Use to wipe rims of jars. Lay a dry towel on the counter to set hot jars on (never directly on the counter; they may crack) or set on a wire rack. And, of course, use them to wipe up spills.

4 COLANDER Useful for washing produce and draining juice from sliced or cut-up produce. Line it with cheesecloth and set over a bowl to finely strain juices for canned juice or jellies.

5 MEASURING CUPS Use measuring cups for dry goods, such as sugar. (Use glass measures for liquids; they measure differently.) Metal is more durable and finely ground food slides out of it more easily with no static cling. Most come in sets of 1 cup, ½ cup, ⅓ cup, and ¼ cup.

6 LADLES Canning involves transferring liquids from one container to another, and a ladle does that quickly and precisely. Metal is ideal because it won't melt if left too close to a burner. If you use plastic, select a black one; light-color plastic tends to stain.

7 TIMER A timer is important for keeping track of cooking and processing times. The timer built into a stove works fine, but a portable timer can be tucked in your pocket while you leave the room.

8 RULER If you don't have a combination ruler/spatula (see page 13), use it to measure headspace when filling jars or when a recipe specifies produce cut in certain lengths.

9 MEASURING SPOONS Most sets have 1 tablespoon, 1 teaspoon, ½ teaspoon, and ¼ teaspoon. Quality metal spoons cost just a bit more and, like metal measuring cups, better release finely ground foods that might otherwise cling.

10 HOT PADS One pair is essential, but two is better so that you always have a clean, dry pair. Or try silicone hot pads—they clean up in a snap.

11 PERMANENT MARKER Use to write on metal, paper, plastic, and glass. Once the ink is dry, it is fairly resistant to fading and moisture.

Create a canner

Today's boiling-water canners are sold with special racks that set the jars submerged in the water or that can be lifted up to rest on the side and hold the jars partially submerged. But you don't have to buy a boiling-water canner to can. If you have a large stockpot that has a well-fitting lid and holds several jars to a few inches deeper than their height, you can use that. You will need a rack to set jars up off the bottom to allow water to flow under them and heat the jars evenly. Make your own rack by wiring together lid rings to fit into the pot.

CANNING INGREDIENTS

Canning uses some specialty ingredients that improve the quality (and, in some cases, safety) of food. Some are as basic as salt—others are more specialized.

Most ingredients for canning are already in your pantry—that's the beauty of home preservation. You aren't using chemicals or additives whose names you can't pronounce and that you don't understand.

That doesn't mean each ingredient isn't important. Each has its role in the canning process, interacting with other ingredients, so don't vary or substitute unless the recipe specifies. A few key specialty ingredients that help ensure quality canned goods:

1 VINEGAR This highly acidic liquid is key to making pickles, salsas, and other preserved goods. Recipes usually specify what type of vinegar to use. However, when in doubt, use white vinegar, which you can purchase by the gallon, because it's clear and won't discolor produce.

Apple cider vinegar is also commonly used in canning recipes.

2 SUGAR Sugar, obviously, helps flavor foods. However, when simmered, it also affects the texture of canned goods, making them thicker. Sugar interacts with pectin, so follow any recipe that calls for both exactly to avoid a preserve that's too thick or too runny. Do not substitute honey unless the recipe specifies it.

3 LIQUID PECTIN Available in a variety of formulations, pectin adds body and gel to jams and jellies. Liquid pectin speeds the dissolving process. Use low-sugar pectins to reduce sugar in jams and preserves. (Follow a low-sugar recipe or follow the directions on the product; don't just reduce the sugar, or texture will be affected.)

4 PECTIN POWDER Use traditional powder types by first mixing them with sugar, then mixing them with the fruit and other ingredients. Stir or cook fruit to dissolve the pectin. Freezer-jam pectins dissolve quickly and create optimal texture in freezer preserves, which tend to be slightly softer than traditional preserves.

5 ASCORBIC ACID COLOR KEEPER This powder protects color and flavor of fruits, such as apples and peaches, and vegetables that darken when peeled or cut.

Dissolve the powder in water. Then briefly soak cut-up produce in the solution.

6 BOTTLED LEMON JUICE Fresh lemon juice and grated lemon peel are added to some recipes for flavor. But in other recipes (such as those containing tomatoes) that just call for lemon juice, use only bottled lemon juice.

In those recipes, lemon juice is added to boost acidity for a safe product. Use bottled lemon juice because it has a consistent acidity, unlike that of fresh lemons, which vary in acidity.

7 SALT A variety of salts can be used in canning recipes, but for best results use canning salt. It has a fine texture and will dissolve readily. Its fine texture also makes it measure differently than coarser salts, so use it for the most accurate measuring in canning recipes. Also, canning salt is free from anticlumping additives that can cause cloudiness in brines.

Salt is one of the few ingredients in canning that you can adjust in all recipes to taste.

Pickling lime

Not to be confused with citrus fruit lime, this powder is made of calcium hydroxide, which improves firmness in pickles. Dissolve the powder in water and soak produce (usually cucumbers) in it for a day or two. Rinse thoroughly several times with repeat soakings to remove excess lime. Use only in recipes that specify its use.

RAW AND HOT PACKS

Food is loaded into jars in one of two ways—the hot-pack or the raw-pack method. Here's how to determine which is better for your situation.

To achieve ideal flavor and texture, a recipe will follow either a hot-pack or raw-pack method.

Although the recipe might not refer to these names, it will instruct you to put food into a jar raw and top it with hot liquid or to cook the food first and pack it, still hot, into jars.

HOT PACK

For food that is firm and processes well, this method is preferred. It's the better method for most fruits and vegetables, meats, poultry, and seafoods.

Simmer food in brine, water, juice, or syrup for a few minutes. Then load the food, still hot, into hot, sterilized jars.

Precooking the food this way breaks it down more to eliminate air so it's less likely to spoil and so food doesn't float. Also more produce can be loaded into fewer jars and processing time is less because the food is already hot—a significant advantage if you're processing large amounts of food.

RAW PACK

Also called cold pack, this method is better for foods that are more delicate and that would have a tough time standing up to a cooking process followed by the heat-intensive canning process.

Food is placed into the jar while still raw and packed in firmly but not crushed. Boiling brine, syrup, juice, or water is added if additional liquid is needed (the recipe will specify).

This method is fast and easy and helps preserve texture. However, it also may result in some shrinkage as food is processed, causing some foods to float to the top of the jar.

With the hot-pack method, food is simmered and then ladled, still hot, into hot jars.

Measuring headspace

The amount of headspace is specified by the recipe and is important to ensure that a jar seals properly.

Measure headspace with a ruler or canning tool from the top of the jar to the top of the liquid. It's okay if a little bit of solid food rises above the liquid; it will settle into the liquid over time.

¼"
½"
1"

PREPARING JARS AND LIDS

Before filling, jars and lids need to be heated and sterilized in the canner or other hot water to ensure safely canned foods. The process isn't difficult, but follow these directions to do it correctly in record time.

STERILIZING JARS

All jars must be cleaned and sterilized before using.

You can simply dip them in a large pan of simmering water for a few minutes and then load them, still hot, with food.

A more efficient way is to use the canner, which already has hot water in it. After filling the canner halfway and bringing the water to just below a simmer, put the jars in it, filling each jar with some hot water to prevent floating. If the canner has an adjustable rack, position it in the highest position. Cover with the lid to get the jars hot and steamy. They don't need to be submerged; the steam will sterilize them. After a few minutes, the jars are ready to fill.

Take out just one jar at a time, fill it, put on the lid, and return it to the canner to keep everything hot. Then take out another jar and fill it: one jar out, one jar in.

HEATING LIDS

Before using lids, heat them to soften the sealing compound. Put the lids in the canner with the jars as you sterilize them. Or heat them in a saucepan by themselves if you wish.

Regardless, the water must be very hot (180°F) to soften the compound but must not boil or the compound will start to break down.

Rings can also be sterilized, but it's not necessary. Instead you can wash them in hot, soapy water and rinse thoroughly.

All about lids

Lids are essentially flat disks of metal with a sticky compound around the edge. When heated, that compound softens, then cools, and creates a long-lasting seal.

Lids also have a raised circle in the center. After canning, if a vacuum seal has been created, that raised circle is sucked down and flattened. If the seal has not been properly created, you can press the circle with your finger and it will pop up and down. (In that case, refrigerate and eat the food within a few to several days.)

The function of bands is simply to hold the lids in place during processing and cooling. They can be reused many times unless they start to rust.

BOILING-WATER CANNING

This method really couldn't be much simpler. Prepare the food and put it in jars, then submerge jars in simmering water for a specified time. Tomatoes are shown here, but the overall steps are the same for other foods.

STEP 1 PREPARE THE FOOD
While you're preparing the food to be canned, heat water in the canner. Fill the canner about halfway with water and position the rack. Set jars in the canner to sterilize (see page 19).

SCORE THE TOMATOES Make an X in the blossom end of each tomato with a small sharp knife.

BLANCH Heat a large kettle of water to boiling. Drop in the tomatoes to simmer for 1 or 2 minutes.

COOL AND PEEL Immediately plunge the tomatoes into icy water to loosen the skins. The skins will slip off easily. Cut out the stem ends with a small, sharp knife.

STEP 2 FILL THE JARS
The cold-pack method for tomatoes is shown here, but follow the exact process specified in the recipe you are following.

FILL Pack the jar as tightly as you can with the food without crushing it. Top with any hot liquid as specified in the recipe.

REMOVE AIR BUBBLES Insert a special canning tool or a thin, flexible spatula down along the sides of the jar to remove any air bubbles. Measure headspace (see page 18), adding or removing liquid as needed.

WIPE Wipe rim and threads of jar with a clean, damp cloth to remove any residue that might interfere with the seal.

PUT ON LID Set lid on jar and screw on band no more than fingertip-tight, just tight enough that you could turn the band another ¼ to ½ inch tighter. This is important for a proper seal.

STEP 3 PROCESS THE JARS

Submerging the jars in boiling water heats and sterilizes the food inside and is the first step in creating a sealed jar.

PLACE JARS IN CANNER As you fill each jar, set it back in the canner filled with simmering water. The canner shown has a rack with handles to hang on the canner rim so that jars sit halfway in the water.

PROCESS JARS When all jars are filled, lower them into the canner. They should be covered with 1 to 2 inches water. Add more boiling water if needed to achieve this. Start processing time from the moment the water starts to boil. Keep at a low, rolling boil.

REMOVE JARS When processing time is up, turn off heat. Using pot holders, lift up the rack and rest handles on the side of the canner. Allow the jars to cool in place for a few minutes.

STEP 4 COOL

Remove jars from canner and set on a wire rack or a towel on the countertop (cold, bare countertops can crack jars). Do not tighten bands. Allow to cool 12 to 24 hours. After that time test the seal by firmly pressing your finger on the center of the lid. It should not give. If it makes a popping sound, it is not properly sealed. Store in the refrigerator and eat the food soon. Otherwise, store jars in a cool, dry place for up to one year.

Of the two methods of canning—boiling-water canning and pressure canning—the former is the simpler of the two. While it may not be as versatile as pressure canning, it is a terrific place to start.

CHAPTER 2

Berries & Cherries

Whether harvested from brambles, bushes, patches, or trees, these tiny ambassadors of summer sweetness share one thing—rich, exotic, and intoxicating taste.

STRAWBERRY-
KUMQUAT JAM

STRAWBERRY AND
GINGER ALE JAM

STRAWBERRY-MARSALA-
THYME JAM

BALSAMIC
STRAWBERRY AND PINK
PEPPERCORN JAM

Strawberry Jam

To distribute the fruit, cool the jam about 20 minutes after processing, then gently turn and tilt the jars without inverting them. Repeat as needed until fruit is well distributed. Jam may need to stand for 1 to 2 weeks after canning to become fully set.

PREP: 40 minutes **PROCESS:** 5 minutes

12 cups strawberries
(3 quarts)
1 1.75-ounce package
regular powdered fruit
pectin
½ teaspoon butter
7 cups sugar

1 Place 1 cup of the strawberries in an 8-quart heavy pot. Using a potato masher, crush berries; continue adding and crushing berries. Measure 5 cups crushed berries. Stir in pectin and butter. Bring to a full rolling boil, stirring constantly. Add sugar all at once. Return to boiling, stirring constantly. Boil hard for 1 minute, stirring constantly. Remove from heat. Skim off foam with a metal spoon.

2 Ladle jam into hot, sterilized half-pint canning jars, leaving a ¼-inch headspace. Wipe jar rims; adjust lids.

3 Process filled jars in a boiling-water canner for 5 minutes (start timing when water returns to boiling). Remove jars from canner; cool on wire racks. **Makes about 10 half-pints.**

PER TABLESPOON: 38 cal., 0 g fat, 0 mg chol., 0 mg sodium, 10 g carbo., 0 g fiber, 0 g pro.

Balsamic Strawberry and Pink Peppercorn Jam: Prepare as directed, except stir in ½ cup balsamic vinegar with the pectin and butter. Stir in ¼ cup pink peppercorns after skimming off foam. Stir before serving.

Strawberry and Ginger Ale Jam: Prepare as directed, except add ½ cup ginger ale after skimming off the foam.

Strawberry-Marsala-Thyme Jam: Prepare as directed, except stir in ½ cup Marsala wine with the butter and pectin. Add ¼ cup fresh snipped thyme after skimming off the foam.

Strawberry-Kumquat Jam: In a small nonreactive heavy saucepan bring 1 cup quartered kumquats (seeds removed) and 1 cup water to boiling; reduce heat. Simmer, covered, for about 20 minutes or until kumquats are tender; drain. Prepare as directed, except reduce the crushed berries to 4 cups and add kumquats to crushed berries.

Strawberry Margarita Jam

Is it a cocktail or an accoutrement? Just one taste of this jewel-tone jam suggests both.

PREP: 35 minutes   **PROCESS:** 5 minutes

3   **cups crushed strawberries
(about 6 cups whole berries)**
⅔   **cup lime juice**
½   **cup tequila**
¼   **cup Triple Sec**
6   **cups sugar**
½   **of a 6-ounce package (1 foil
pouch) liquid fruit pectin**
1   **teaspoon finely shredded
lime peel**

1 In an 8- to 10-quart heavy pot combine strawberries, lime juice, tequila, and Triple Sec. Gradually add sugar, stirring to combine. Bring to a full rolling boil, stirring constantly. Quickly stir in pectin and lime peel. Return to a full rolling boil, stirring constantly. Boil hard for 1 minute. Remove from heat. Quickly skim off foam with a metal spoon.

2 Ladle hot jam into hot, sterilized half-pint canning jars, leaving a ¼-inch headspace. Wipe jar rims; adjust lids.

3 Process filled jars in a boiling-water canner for 5 minutes (start timing when water returns to boiling). Remove jars from canner; cool on wire racks. To distribute fruit, cool for about 20 minutes, then gently turn and tilt jars without inverting them; repeat as needed. **Makes 7 half-pints.**

PER TABLESPOON: 47 cal., 0 g fat, 0 mg chol., 0 mg sodium, 11 g carbo., 0 g fiber, 0 g pro.

tip

Check with a farmer's market or call local growers to find out when strawberries are at their peak in your area. Typically they peak as early as March in the South and as late as July in the North.

Can It!

Strawberry-Rhubarb Freezer Jam

The tartness of rhubarb offers a lovely balance to the sweetness of the ripe strawberries. Try this delicious jam on tart Greek yogurt drizzled with honey and sprinkled with granola.

PREP: 25 minutes **STAND:** 10 minutes + 24 hours

3 cups strawberries
1 cup finely chopped rhubarb
5 cups sugar
½ teaspoon finely shredded lemon peel
¾ cup water
1 1.75-ounce package regular powdered fruit pectin

1 In a large bowl crush berries using a potato masher. Measure 1½ cups crushed berries. Stir in rhubarb. Add sugar and lemon peel; stir to combine. Allow to stand at room temperature for 10 minutes, stirring occasionally.

2 In a small saucepan combine the water and pectin. Bring to boiling, stirring constantly. Boil hard for 1 minute, stirring constantly. Remove from heat. Add pectin mixture to fruit mixture, stirring for about 3 minutes or until sugar dissolves and mixture is no longer grainy.

3 Ladle hot jam into half-pint freezer containers, leaving a ½-inch headspace. Seal and label. Let stand at room temperature for about 24 hours or until set. Store for up to 3 weeks in the refrigerator or for up to 1 year in the freezer. **Makes 5 half-pints.**

PER TABLESPOON: 53 cal., 0 g fat, 0 mg chol., 1 mg sodium, 14 g carbo., 0 g fiber, 0 g pro.

TEST KITCHEN
tip

Because the fruit mixture in this recipe is cooked, you can use regular powdered fruit pectin. For no-cook freezer-jam recipes, use freezer jam pectin, which is specifically made to dissolve easily and gel well in no-cook preserves recipes.

Brandied Strawberry Freezer Jam

Serve this elegant jam alongside your favorite fried pastry or fritter—or slathered on a croissant.

PREP: 35 minutes   **STAND:** 10 minutes + 24 hours

4	cups strawberries
4	cups sugar
3	tablespoons brandy
½	teaspoon finely shredded lemon peel
1	1.75-ounce package regular powdered fruit pectin
¾	cup water

1 In a large bowl crush the strawberries using a potato masher. Measure 2 cups crushed berries; stir in sugar, brandy, and lemon peel. Let stand at room temperature for 10 minutes, stirring occasionally.

2 In a small saucepan stir pectin into the water. Bring to boiling, stirring constantly. Boil hard for 1 minute, stirring constantly. Remove from heat. Stir pectin mixture into berry mixture, stirring for about 3 minutes or until sugar dissolves and mixture is no longer grainy.

3 Ladle hot jam into half-pint freezer containers, leaving a ½-inch headspace. Seal and label.

4 Let stand at room temperature for about 24 hours or until set. Store for up to 3 weeks in the refrigerator or for up to 1 year in the freezer. **Makes 5 half-pints.**

PER TABLESPOON: 45 cal., 0 g fat, 0 mg chol., 1 mg sodium, 11 g carbo., 0 g fiber, 0 g pro.

When you work with dark red, blue, or black fruits, wear dark colors. The roly-poly fruits really stain.

Strawberry-Lemon Marmalade

Special marmalades like this one make a delectable alternative to syrup on pancakes.

PREP: 55 minutes   **COOK:** 30 minutes   **PROCESS:** 5 minutes   **STAND:** 2 weeks

2   medium lemons
½   cup water
⅛   teaspoon baking soda
3   cups crushed strawberries
    (about 6 cups whole berries)
5   cups sugar
½   of a 6-ounce package (1 foil
    pouch) liquid fruit pectin

1 Score the peel of each lemon into four lengthwise sections; remove the peels with your fingers. Using a sharp knife, scrape off the white portions of peels; discard. Cut peels into thin strips.

2 In a large saucepan combine peel strips, the water, and baking soda. Bring to boiling; reduce heat. Simmer, covered, for 20 minutes. Do not drain. Section lemons, reserving juice; discard seeds. Add lemon sections and juice to peel strips mixture. Stir in crushed strawberries. Return to boiling; reduce heat. Simmer, covered, for 10 minutes (you should have about 3 cups mixture).

3 In an 8- to 10-quart heavy pot combine lemon-strawberry mixture and sugar. Bring to a full rolling boil, stirring constantly. Quickly stir in pectin. Return to a full rolling boil, stirring constantly. Boil hard for 1 minute, stirring constantly. Remove from heat. Quickly skim off foam with a metal spoon.

4 Ladle hot marmalade into hot, sterilized half-pint canning jars, leaving a ¼-inch headspace. Wipe jar rims; adjust lids.

5 Process filled jars in a boiling-water canner for 5 minutes (start timing when water returns to boiling). Remove jars from canner; cool on wire racks. Allow to set at room temperature for 2 weeks before serving. **Makes 6 half-pints.**

PER TABLESPOON: 44 cal., 0 g fat, 0 mg chol., 2 mg sodium, 11 g carbo., 0 g fiber, 0 g pro.

Raspberry Jam

You can cut the sweetness of this jam by stirring 2 tablespoons lemon juice into the fruit mixture before ladling it into jars

PREP: 35 minutes **PROCESS:** 5 minutes

8 **cups raspberries**
1 **1.75-ounce package regular powdered fruit pectin**
7 **cups sugar**

1 In an 8- to 10-quart heavy pot crush 1 cup of the raspberries using a potato masher. Continue adding berries and crushing until you have 5 cups crushed berries. Stir in pectin. Bring to a full rolling boil, stirring constantly. Stir sugar all at once into berry mixture. Return to a full rolling boil, stirring constantly. Boil hard for 1 minute, stirring constantly. Remove from heat. Quickly skim off foam with a metal spoon.

2 Ladle hot jam into hot, sterilized half-pint canning jars, leaving a ¼-inch headspace. Wipe jar rims; adjust lids.

3 Process filled jars in a boiling-water canner for 5 minutes (start timing when the water returns to boiling). Remove jars from canner; cool on wire racks. **Makes 8 half-pints.**

PER TABLESPOON: 46 cal., 0 g fat, 0 mg chol., 1 mg sodium, 12 g carbo., 1 g fiber, 0 g pro.

TEST KITCHEN TIP: You can jazz up a basic fruit jam such as this one by adding one of the following to the fruit mixture along with the sugar: 1 teaspoon finely shredded lemon peel, ½ teaspoon ground nutmeg, or ¼ teaspoon grated fresh ginger.

Blackberry Jam

Although this jam takes toast to new heights, there are so many other uses for it. Try it as a filling in a thumbprint cookie. On the savory side, its rich flavor also complements sage-roasted pork.

PREP: 35 minutes   **PROCESS:** 5 minutes

3	cups blackberries
⅓	cup sugar
¼	cup sorghum or molasses
3	tablespoons blackberry brandy or orange juice
¼	cup orange juice
3	tablespoons cornstarch

1 In a large heavy saucepan combine blackberries, sugar, sorghum, and brandy. Bring to boiling; reduce heat. Simmer, uncovered, for 5 minutes, stirring occasionally.

2 In a small bowl stir the ¼ cup orange juice into the cornstarch. Stir orange mixture into berry mixture in saucepan. Cook and stir over medium heat until thickened and bubbly. Cook and stir for 2 minutes more. Cool for 15 minutes.

3 Ladle jam into an airtight storage container. Seal and label. Store in the refrigerator for up to 2 weeks. **Makes about 2 cups.**

PER TABLESPOON: 49 cal., 0 g fat, 0 mg chol., 5 mg sodium, 0 g carbo., 0 g fiber, 0 g pro.

Spiced Blueberry Jam

Make PB&J sandwich cookies by spreading this jam between two peanut butter cookies.

PREP: 30 minutes   **PROCESS:** 5 minutes

6	cups blueberries
2	tablespoons lemon juice
½	teaspoon ground cinnamon
¼	teaspoon ground allspice
	Dash ground cloves
7	cups sugar
1	6-ounce package (2 foil pouches) liquid fruit pectin

1 Place the blueberries in an 8- to 10-quart heavy pot. Crush blueberries using a potato masher. Measure 4½ cups crushed berries. Stir lemon juice, cinnamon, allspice, and cloves into blueberries. Stir in sugar.

2 Bring mixture to a rolling boil, stirring constantly. Stir in pectin. Return to a rolling boil, stirring constantly. Boil hard for 1 minute, stirring constantly. Remove from heat. Skim off foam with a metal spoon.

3 Ladle hot jam into hot, sterilized half-pint canning jars, leaving a ¼-inch headspace. Wipe jar rims; adjust lids.

4 Process filled jars in a boiling-water canner for 5 minutes (start timing when water returns to boiling). Remove jars from canner; cool on wire racks. **Makes 9 half-pints.**

PER TABLESPOON: 41 cal., 0 g fat, 0 mg chol., 1 mg sodium, 11 g carbo., 0 g pro.

Cinnamon, allspice, and cloves enhance the subtle flavor of blueberries. For classic blueberry jam, simply omit the spices.

Blackberry-Port Jam

The dark, sweet essences of blackberries taste wonderful simply spread on warm, fresh-from-the-oven biscuits.

PREP: 35 minutes   **PROCESS:** 5 minutes

4	cups blackberries
5½	cups sugar
1	1.75-ounce package regular powdered fruit pectin
1	cup vintage port
¼	teaspoon ground cloves

1 Place the blackberries in an 8- to 10-quart heavy pot. Using a potato masher, crush the berries slightly. In a small bowl combine ¼ cup of the sugar and the pectin; gradually stir into the berries. Stir in port and cloves.

2 Bring to a full rolling boil, stirring constantly. Add the remaining 5¼ cups sugar. Return to a full rolling boil, stirring constantly. Boil, uncovered, for 1 minute or until jam sheets off a metal spoon (see tip, page 177), stirring constantly. Remove from heat. Skim off foam with a metal spoon.

3 Ladle hot jam into hot, sterilized half-pint canning jars, leaving a ¼-inch headspace. Wipe jar rims; adjust lids. (Place any extra jam in an airtight container and store in refrigerator for up 2 weeks.)

4 Process filled jars in a boiling-water canner for 5 minutes (start timing when water returns to boiling). Remove jars from canner; cool on wire racks until set. **Makes 6 half-pints.**

PER TABLESPOON: 51 cal., 0 g fat, 0 mg chol., 0 mg sodium, 12 g carbo., 0 g fiber, 0 g pro.

TEST KITCHEN *tip*

Locally grown blackberries are at their peak in June in the South and July in the North. These black beauties are best for preserving when they are plump, firm, and fully black.

Can It!

Blueberry-Maple-Pecan Conserve

A conserve is a chunky mixture of fruits, nuts, and sugar. Like jams and preserves, conserves are fabulous spread on breads, but they're equally at home on top of a warm baked Brie.

PREP: 20 minutes   **COOK:** 35 minutes   **PROCESS:** 10 minutes

4   cups blueberries
1   cup water
1   cup pure maple syrup
2   tablespoons lemon juice
2   cups packed brown sugar
1   cup dried currants
1   cup chopped pecans
1   teaspoon ground cinnamon

1 In a 4- to 6-quart heavy pot combine blueberries, the water, maple syrup, and lemon juice. Using a potato masher, slightly crush the blueberries. Bring to boiling; reduce heat. Simmer, covered, for about 5 minutes or until blueberries are tender, stirring occasionally.

2 Stir brown sugar and currants into blueberry mixture. Return to boiling, stirring until sugar dissolves; reduce heat. Simmer, uncovered, for about 30 minutes or until mixture thickens, stirring occasionally. Remove from heat. Stir in pecans and cinnamon.

3 Ladle hot conserve into hot, sterilized half-pint canning jars, leaving a ¼-inch headspace. Wipe jar rims; adjust lids.

4 Process in a boiling-water canner for 10 minutes (start timing when water returns to boiling). Remove jars from canner; cool on wire racks. **Makes 5 half-pints.**

PER 2 TABLESPOONS: 100 cal., 2 g fat (0 g sat. fat), 0 mg chol., 4 mg sodium, 21 g carbo., 1 g fiber, 1 g pro.

TEST KITCHEN
tip

Although it is pricey, use pure maple syrup in this recipe—not the corn syrup-based variety. The intensity of the maple flavor is worth every penny.

Honey-Bourbon Pickled Blueberries

These roly-poly orbs of deliciousness are perfectly paired with roast or grilled pork, whether it's chops, ribs, or a roast.

PREP: 35 minutes   **STAND:** 8 to 12 hours   **PROCESS:** 10 minutes

3	inches stick cinnamon
1	teaspoon whole allspice
1¼	cups white wine vinegar
8	cups blueberries
¼	cup bourbon
1¾	cups honey

1 For a spice bag, place cinnamon and allspice in the center of a double-thick, 6-inch square of 100%-cotton cheesecloth. Bring up corners; tie closed with clean kitchen string.

2 In a 4- to 6-quart stainless-steel, enamel, or nonstick heavy pot combine vinegar and spice bag. Bring to boiling; reduce heat. Simmer, covered, for 5 minutes. Add blueberries and bourbon. Cook over medium heat for about 8 minutes or just until syrup is heated through, gently shaking the pot (to avoid breaking the berries, do not stir). Remove from heat; cover and let stand at room temperature for 8 to 12 hours.

3 Remove spice bag; discard. Pour the blueberry mixture into a colander set over a large bowl; reserve liquid.

4 Ladle hot blueberries into hot, sterilized half-pint canning jars, leaving a ½-inch headspace.

5 For syrup, return the reserved liquid to the pot; stir in honey. Bring to boiling, stirring occasionally. Boil, uncovered, for about 5 minutes or until the syrup is slightly thickened. Ladle hot syrup over blueberries, leaving a ½-inch headspace. Wipe jar rims; adjust lids. Discard any remaining syrup.

6 Process filled jars in a boiling-water canner for 10 minutes (start timing when water returns to boiling). Remove jars from canner; cool on wire racks. **Makes 6 half-pints.**

PER ¼ CUP: 112 cal., 0 g fat, 0 mg chol., 2 mg sodium, 27 g carbo., 1 g fiber, 0 g pro.

Cherry-Berry Freezer Jam

This ruby-color jam is beautiful—and tasty—spread over warm corn bread.

PREP: 35 minutes   **STAND:** 10 minutes + 24 hours

1   **pound tart red cherries**
1   **cup mashed blueberries**
4   **cups sugar**
½   **teaspoon finely shredded**
    lemon peel
1   **1.75-ounce package regular**
    powdered fruit pectin
¾   **cup water**

1 Stem, pit, and finely chop cherries. Measure 1½ cups chopped cherries. In a large bowl combine the 1½ cups chopped cherries and mashed blueberries; stir in sugar and lemon peel. Allow to stand at room temperature for 10 minutes, stirring occasionally.

2 In a small saucepan stir pectin into the water. Bring to boiling, stirring constantly. Boil hard for 1 minute, stirring constantly. Remove from heat. Quickly stir pectin mixture into fruit mixture, stirring for about 3 minutes or until sugar dissolves and mixture is no longer grainy.

3 Ladle hot jam into half-pint freezer containers, leaving a ½-inch headspace. Seal and label.

4 Let stand at room temperature for about 24 hours or until set. Store for up to 3 weeks in the refrigerator or for up to 1 year in the freezer. **Makes 5 half-pints.**

PER TABLESPOON: 45 cal., 0 g fat, 0 mg chol., 1 mg sodium, 11 g carbo., 0 g fiber, 0 g pro.

TEST KITCHEN
tip

A cherry pitter, available from a cookware shop, catalog, or online, easily removes pits from cherries. If you don't have a pitter, halve the cherries, then pry out the pits with the tip of a knife.

Sour Cherry and Amaretto Jelly

Whether you are working with sweet or tart red cherries, the marks of good-quality fruit are the same. Look for chubby fruit with glossy skin and deep color. Avoid mushy, dull, or shriveled fruit—and discard any cherries with cracked or split skin.

PREP: 45 minutes **COOK:** 10 minutes **STAND:** 20 minutes **CHILL:** 4 to 12 hours **PROCESS:** 5 minutes

3½	**pounds tart red cherries, pitted**
½	**cup water**
5	**cups granulated sugar**
2	**cups packed brown sugar**
1	**tablespoon lemon juice**
1	**6-ounce package (2 foil pouches) liquid fruit pectin**
½	**cup amaretto**

1 In an 8-quart stainless-steel, enamel, or nonstick heavy pot combine cherries and the water. Bring to boiling, stirring occasionally; reduce heat. Simmer gently, covered, for 10 minutes. Remove from heat; mash with a potato masher. Let stand for 20 minutes.

2 Place a fine-mesh sieve over a large bowl. Ladle the cherries into the sieve and drain juice. Discard pulp and rinse the sieve. Fold a piece of damp 100%-cotton cheesecloth to fit the sieve. Strain cherry juice through the cheesecloth-lined sieve; rinse cheesecloth to remove any sediment and strain juice again. Cover juice and chill for 4 to 12 hours to allow remaining sediment to settle to the bottom of the bowl.

3 Fold another piece of damp cheesecloth to fit the sieve. Strain the cherry juice through the cheesecloth-lined sieve, being careful not to disturb the sediment at the bottom of the bowl.

4 In the same 8-quart pot combine 3½ cups of the cherry juice (save any remaining cherry juice for another use), the granulated sugar, brown sugar, and lemon juice. Bring to boiling over medium heat, stirring constantly until sugars dissolve.

5 Increase heat to medium-high; bring mixture to a full rolling boil, stirring constantly. Stir in pectin. Return to a full rolling boil, stirring constantly. Boil for 1 minute more. Remove from heat. Stir in amaretto. Quickly skim off foam with a metal spoon.

6 Ladle hot jelly into hot, sterilized half-pint canning jars, leaving a ¼-inch headspace. Wipe jar rims; adjust lids.

7 Process filled jars in a boiling-water canner for 5 minutes (start timing when water returns to boiling). Remove jars from canner; cool on wire racks. **Makes 8 half-pints.**

PER TABLESPOON: 48 cal., 0 g fat, 0 mg chol., 1 mg sodium, 12 g carbo., 0 g fiber, 0 g pro.

Vanilla-Scented Pickled Sweet Cherries

One bite reveals that life is truly a bowl of cherries. Feeling indulgent? Pop one of the cherries into a vodka martini for an after-dinner treat.

PREP: 25 minutes   **STAND:** 8 to 12 hours + 3 days   **COOK:** 15 minutes   **CHILL:** 1 month

4	cups sweet cherries
2	cups white balsamic vinegar
1	cup sugar
1	cup water
1	vanilla bean, split lengthwise
3	inches stick cinnamon
1	tablespoon kirsch (optional)
2	teaspoons almond extract

1 Sort and wash cherries. If desired, stem and pit cherries. In a large nonmetal bowl combine cherries and vinegar. Cover the bowl and let stand at room temperature for 8 to 12 hours.

2 Drain the vinegar from the cherries into a medium stainless-steel, enamel, or nonstick saucepan. Add sugar, the water, vanilla bean, and stick cinnamon. Bring to boiling, stirring until sugar dissolves; reduce heat to low. Simmer, uncovered, for 15 minutes. Remove from heat; let cool.

3 Stir the kirsch (if using) and almond extract into the cooled vinegar mixture. Pour over cherries. Cover and let stand at room temperature for 3 days.

4 Drain the liquid into a medium stainless-steel, enamel, or nonstick saucepan, discarding vanilla bean pieces and cinnamon stick. Bring to boiling. Remove from heat. Strain liquid; let cool.

5 Meanwhile, pack the cherries into sterilized half-pint jars. Pour liquid over cherries in jars, filling the jars to the brims. Seal with nonreactive lids. Refrigerate for at least 1 month before serving. **Makes 5 half-pints.**

PER ¼ CUP: 83 cal., 0 g fat, 0 mg chol., 6 mg sodium, 19 g carbo., 1 g fiber, 0 g pro.

Sweet cherries, such as Bing and Rainier cherries, have a relatively short growing season, from early June to mid-August.

CHAPTER 3

Totally Tomatoes

When charming pendants of plump, ruby-color tomatoes ripen to perfection, capture their heavenly flavor and irresistible juiciness in sparkling jars.

Tomato-Basil Simmer Sauce

Kids love this sweetly delicious tomato sauce. Toss it with spaghetti and frozen meatballs for a quick dinner.

PREP: 2 hours   **COOK:** 1 hour 10 minutes   **PROCESS:** 35 minutes

12   pounds ripe tomatoes, peeled
      (see tip, page 61)
3   tablespoons packed
      brown sugar
2   tablespoons kosher salt
1   tablespoon balsamic vinegar
1   teaspoon freshly ground
      black pepper
2   cups lightly packed fresh basil
      leaves, snipped
1   cup lightly packed assorted
      fresh herbs (such as oregano,
      thyme, and/or Italian
      [flat-leaf]) parsley, snipped
1   tablespoon crushed red pepper
      (optional)
6   tablespoons lemon juice

1 Cut peeled tomatoes into chunks and add some of the chunks to a food processor. Cover and process until chopped. Transfer chopped tomatoes to a 7- to 8-quart stainless-steel, enamel, or nonstick heavy pot. Repeat chopping remaining tomatoes, in batches, in the food processor. Add all tomatoes to the pot.

2 Add brown sugar, salt, vinegar, and black pepper to the tomatoes. Bring to boiling, stirring often; reduce heat. Simmer, uncovered, for 70 to 80 minutes or until mixture is reduced to about 11 cups and is desired sauce consistency, stirring occasionally. Remove from heat; stir in basil and other herbs and, if desired, crushed red pepper.

3 Spoon 1 tablespoon of the lemon juice into each hot, sterilized pint canning jar. Ladle hot sauce into jars with lemon juice, leaving a ½-inch headspace. Wipe jar rims; adjust lids.

4 Process filled jars in a boiling-water canner for 35 minutes (start timing when water returns to boiling). Remove jars from canner; cool on wire racks. **Makes 6 pints.**

PER ½ CUP: 57 cal., 1 g fat (0 g sat. fat), 0 mg chol., 539 mg sodium, 13 g carbo., 3 g fiber, 2 g pro.

Double-Tomato Simmer Sauce: Prepare as directed above, except stir in 1 cup snipped dried tomatoes (not oil pack) with the herbs.

Pickled Pear Tomatoes with Rosemary

For a simple but superb appetizer, serve with sliced baguette. If you like, toast the bread and spread with a little bit of soft goat cheese.

PREP: 35 minutes   **COOK:** 10 minutes   **PROCESS:** 15 minutes

5	cups yellow and/or red pear-shape or round cherry tomatoes
1	cup thinly slivered sweet onion (such as Vidalia or Walla Walla)
½	teaspoon crushed red pepper
6	cloves garlic, thinly sliced
2¼	cups white balsamic vinegar
¾	cup water
⅓	cup sugar
3	tablespoons pickling salt
1	tablespoon fresh rosemary leaves
½	teaspoon whole black peppercorns
½	teaspoon whole pink peppercorns
½	teaspoon whole white peppercorns
1	bay leaf

1 Wash tomatoes. In a large bowl combine tomatoes, onion, crushed red pepper, and garlic; toss gently to combine. Set aside.

2 In a large stainless-steel, enamel, or nonstick heavy saucepan combine vinegar, the water, sugar, salt, rosemary, black peppercorns, pink peppercorns, white peppercorns, and bay leaf. Bring to boiling, stirring until sugar dissolves; reduce heat. Simmer, uncovered, for 10 minutes, stirring often. Remove and discard bay leaf.

3 Pack tomato mixture into hot, sterilized half-pint canning jars, leaving a ½-inch headspace. Pour hot vinegar mixture over tomato mixture in jars, maintaining the ½-inch headspace. Remove any air bubbles in jars. Wipe jar rims; adjust lids.

4 Process filled jars in a boiling-water canner for 15 minutes (start timing when water returns to boiling). Remove jars from canner; cool on wire racks. **Makes 7 half-pints.**

PER ¼ CUP: 34 cal., 0 g fat (0 g sat. fat), 0 mg chol., 631 mg sodium, 7 g carbo., 0 g fiber, 0 g pro.

Because tomatoes come in early-season, midseason, and late-season varieties, the canning season may last 90 days. In most areas, tomatoes are harvested from mid- to late June through early autumn. Often, the most flavorful varieties ripen last.

Spicy Pickled Green Tomatoes

This spicy-sweet condiment tastes amazing on saucy pulled chicken or pork sandwiches. It's a great late-season recipe to put up when there are still tomatoes on the vine but the weather is cool enough that they are not ripening.

PREP: 1 hour   **PROCESS:** 15 minutes

3	pounds green tomatoes
3	medium onions, sliced
½	cup seeded, chopped red sweet pepper (1 small)
¼	cup seeded, finely chopped fresh jalapeño chile peppers* (4 medium)
4½	cups white vinegar
3	cups sugar
2	tablespoons mustard seeds
5	teaspoons whole black peppercorns
2	teaspoons celery seeds

1 Wash and core tomatoes. Remove stems. Cut tomatoes into ¼-inch-thick slices. Measure 12 cups tomato slices. In a large bowl combine the 12 cups tomatoes, the onion slices, sweet pepper, and chile peppers; set aside.

2 In a large stainless-steel, enamel, or nonstick heavy saucepan combine vinegar, sugar, mustard seeds, peppercorns, and celery seeds. Bring to boiling, stirring until sugar dissolves. Remove from heat.

3 Pack tomato mixture into hot, sterilized pint canning jars, leaving a ½-inch headspace. Pour hot vinegar mixture over tomato mixture in jars, maintaining the ½-inch headspace. Wipe jar rims; adjust lids.

4 Process in a boiling-water canner for 15 minutes (start timing when water returns to boiling). Remove jars from canner; cool on wire racks. **Makes 6 pints.**

PER ¼ CUP: 71 cal., 0 g fat, 0 mg chol., 5 mg sodium, 19 g carbo., 0 g fiber, 1 g pro.

*TEST KITCHEN TIP: Because chile peppers contain volatile oils that can burn your skin and eyes, avoid direct contact with them as much as possible. When working with chile peppers, wear plastic or rubber gloves. If your bare hands do touch the peppers, wash your hands and nails well with soap and warm water.

Chunky Homemade Salsa

The peppers you choose vary the spiciness of this salsa. Anaheims and jalapeños give you a fairly mild salsa. Turn up the heat with poblanos and serranos.

PREP: 1 hour 30 minutes **STAND:** 30 minutes **COOK:** 1 hour 40 minutes **PROCESS:** 15 minutes

8	**pounds ripe tomatoes**
2	**cups seeded and chopped fresh Anaheim or poblano chile peppers (2 to 3) (see tip, page 57)**
⅓	**to ½ cup seeded and chopped fresh jalapeño or serrano chile peppers (2 large) (see tip, page 57)**
2	**cups chopped onions (2 large)**
½	**cup snipped fresh cilantro or parsley**
½	**cup lime juice**
½	**cup white vinegar**
½	**of a 6-ounce can tomato paste (⅓ cup)**
5	**cloves garlic, minced**
1	**teaspoon salt**
1	**teaspoon cumin seeds, toasted and crushed**
1	**teaspoon black pepper**

1 Wash tomatoes. Remove stem ends. To peel tomatoes, bring 4 inches of water to boiling in a large saucepan. Immerse tomatoes, a few at a time, into boiling water for 30 to 60 seconds or until the skins start to crack. Immediately dip tomatoes into cold water; drain in a colander. Slip off skins; discard. Remove cores and seeds. Coarsely chop tomatoes. Measure 15 cups chopped tomatoes; place in a large colander set in sink. Allow to stand for 30 minutes.

2 Transfer tomatoes to a 7- to 8-quart stainless-steel, enamel, or nonstick heavy pot. Bring to boiling; reduce heat. Simmer, uncovered, for about 1½ hours or until tomatoes are desired consistency, stirring often.

3 Add chiles, onions, cilantro, lime juice, vinegar, tomato paste, garlic, salt, cumin seeds, and black pepper. Return mixture to boiling; reduce heat. Simmer, uncovered, for 10 minutes. Remove from heat.

4 Ladle hot salsa into hot, sterilized pint canning jars, leaving a ½-inch headspace. Wipe jar rims; adjust lids.

5 Process filled jars in a boiling-water canner for 15 minutes (start timing when water returns to boiling). Remove jars from canner; cool on wire racks. **Makes about 5 pints.**

PER 2 TABLESPOONS: 13 cal., 0 g fat, 0 mg chol., 40 mg sodium, 3 g carbo., 1 g fiber, 1 g pro.

Hot Chipotle Salsa: Prepare as directed, except omit jalapeño chile peppers. Stir in 7 ounces (1 can) chipotle peppers in adobo sauce, chopped, with the Anaheim chile peppers.

Green Salsa: Prepare as directed, except substitute 15 cups chopped green tomatoes for the red tomatoes and omit standing time and tomato paste. Bring tomatoes to boiling and cook for 15 to 20 minutes, stirring frequently. After adding the chile peppers and other ingredients, cook mixture, covered, for 10 minutes, stirring frequently.

Tomato-Basil Jam

Slather this tasty spread on warm focaccia for an easy appetizer or use it to pump up the flavor of a baked cheese sandwich.

PREP: 30 minutes   **COOK:** 11 minutes   **PROCESS:** 5 minutes

2½   **pounds ripe tomatoes, peeled (see tip, below)**
¼   **cup lemon juice**
3   **tablespoons snipped fresh basil**
3   **cups sugar**
1   **1.75-ounce package powdered fruit pectin for lower-sugar recipes**

1   Seed, core, and finely chop tomatoes. Measure 3½ cups chopped tomatoes; place in a 6- to 8-quart stainless-steel, enamel, or nonstick heavy pot. Bring to boiling, stirring occasionally; reduce heat. Simmer, covered, for 10 minutes, stirring often. Measure 3⅓ cups tomatoes. Return to the same pot. Stir in lemon juice and basil.

2   In a small bowl combine ¼ cup of the sugar and the pectin; stir into tomato mixture. Bring to a full rolling boil, stirring constantly. Stir in the remaining 2¾ cups sugar. Return to a full rolling boil, stirring constantly. Boil hard for 1 minute, stirring constantly. Remove from heat. Quickly skim off foam with a metal spoon.

3   Ladle hot jam into hot, sterilized half-pint canning jars, leaving a ¼-inch headspace. Wipe jar rims; adjust lids.

4   Process filled jars in a boiling-water canner for 5 minutes (start timing when water returns to boiling). Remove jars from canner; cool on wire racks. **Makes 5 half-pints.**

PER TABLESPOON: 39 cal., 0 g fat, 0 mg chol., 4 mg sodium, 10 g carbo., 0 g fiber, 0 g pro.

TEST KITCHEN tip

To peel tomatoes, make an ⊠ in the blossom end of each tomato with a small sharp knife. Drop the tomatoes in a large kettle of boiling water and let simmer for 1 or 2 minutes. Immediately plunge the tomatoes in icy water to loosen skins, then peel.

Roasted Tomato and Red Pepper Pizza Sauce

Roasting the peppers, onions, and garlic caramelizes their sugars, creating a natural sweetness in this awesome sauce. A splash of red wine and a little bit of molasses further deepen the flavor.

PREP: 1 hour   **ROAST:** 30 minutes at 450°F   **STAND:** 15 minutes   **COOK:** 40 minutes   **PROCESS:** 35 minutes

8	**pounds ripe plum tomatoes**
3	**pounds red sweet peppers**
8	**cloves garlic, peeled**
¼	**cup full-bodied red wine**
¼	**cup molasses**
1	**tablespoon sugar**
2	**tablespoons kosher salt**
½	**cup lightly packed fresh basil, snipped**
½	**cup lightly packed fresh oregano, snipped**
½	**cup lightly packed Italian (flat-leaf) parsley, snipped**
½	**teaspoon black pepper**
¼	**to ½ teaspoon crushed red pepper**
½	**cup lemon juice**

1 Preheat oven to 450°F. Line one very large roasting pan or two medium roasting pans with parchment paper and one large baking sheet with foil. Cut one or two small slits in each tomato. Place tomatoes in a single layer onto the prepared roasting pan(s). Halve the sweet peppers lengthwise; remove the stems, seeds, and membranes. Place pepper halves, cut sides down, on the foil-lined baking sheet. Scatter garlic cloves around the peppers. Roast the tomatoes, peppers, and garlic for 30 minutes or until tomato skins are blistered, pepper skins are browned, and garlic cloves are lightly browned.

2 Bring foil up around peppers and garlic to enclose. Let stand about 15 minutes. Let tomatoes cool until easy to handle. Coarsely chop the tomatoes, discarding any excess juice and removing any loose skins. Transfer tomatoes to a large stainless-steel, enamel, or nonstick heavy pot. When the peppers are cool enough to handle, gently pull off any loose skins and discard. Coarsely chop the peppers and garlic; add to the tomatoes in pot. Stir in the red wine, molasses, sugar, and salt. Bring to boiling over medium-high heat, stirring occasionally. Reduce heat to low and simmer, uncovered, for 15 minutes.

3 Working in batches, transfer the tomato mixture to a food processor or blender. Cover and process or blend until smooth. Strain processed or blended mixture through a fine-mesh sieve, pushing the liquid through and scraping the inside of the sieve using a rubber spatula; discard solids. Repeat with the remaining mixture.

4 Return the strained mixture to the large pot. Stir in the fresh herbs, black pepper, and crushed red pepper. Bring mixture to boiling; reduce heat. Simmer, uncovered, for 25 minutes or until reduced to 8 cups. Remove from heat and stir in lemon juice.

5 Ladle hot sauce into hot, sterilized half-pint canning jars, leaving a ½-inch headspace. Wipe jar rims; adjust lids.

6 Process filled jars in a boiling-water canner for 35 minutes (start timing when water returns to boiling). Remove jars from canner; cool on wire racks. **Makes 8 half-pints.**

PER 2 TABLESPOONS: 24 cal., 0 g fat, 0 mg chol., 189 mg sodium, 5 g carbo., 1 g fiber, 1 g pro.

Can It!

Spicy Garlic Marinara

Some like it hot! This lip-tingling tomato sauce is delicious on all kinds of pasta. Adjust the heat level with the number of chile peppers you use.

PREP: 1 hour   **COOK:** 1 hour 15 minutes to 1 hour 30 minutes   **PROCESS:** 35 minutes

12	pounds ripe tomatoes, peeled (see tip, page 61)
⅓	cup very finely minced fresh garlic
3	to 5 fresh red cayenne or Thai chile peppers, minced (see tip, page 57)
3	tablespoons sugar
3	tablespoons kosher salt
2	cups lightly packed fresh basil, snipped
½	cup snipped fresh Italian (flat-leaf) parsley
6	tablespoons lemon juice

1 Coarsely chop the peeled tomatoes and transfer to an 8- to 10-quart stainless-steel, enamel, or nonstick heavy pot. Stir in garlic, chile peppers, sugar, and salt. Bring to boiling, stirring often. Reduce heat and simmer, uncovered, for 1¼ to 1½ hours until reduced to 11 to 11½ cups, stirring occasionally. Remove from heat and stir in basil and parsley.

2 Spoon 1 tablespoon of the lemon juice into each hot, sterilized pint canning jar. Ladle hot sauce into jars with lemon juice, leaving a ½-inch headspace. Wipe jar rims; adjust lids.

3 Process filled jars in a boiling-water canner for 35 minutes (start timing when water returns to boiling). Remove jars from canner; cool on wire racks. **Makes 6 pints.**

PER ½ CUP: 54 cal., 1 g fat, 0 mg chol., 751 mg sodium, 12 g carbo., 3 g fiber, 2 g pro.

TEST KITCHEN tip

This recipe calls for ⅓ cup of finely minced garlic—that's a lot of cloves to peel! To easily remove the skin from a garlic clove, place the clove on a cutting board, then lay the broad side of a chef's knife on top of it. Give the knife a firm hit with your fist—the skin should crack and easily peel off.

Fire-Roasted Tomato-Ancho Taco Sauce

This tasty sauce is terrific as a condiment on beef, pork, or chicken tacos and burritos. Or stir a little bit into a pot of pinto or black beans for a flavor boost.

PREP: 35 minutes **BROIL:** 8 to 10 minutes **COOK:** 40 minutes **STAND:** 30 minutes **PROCESS:** 35 minutes

4	pounds plum tomatoes
1	teaspoon cumin seeds
8	ounces fresh poblano peppers, seeded and chopped (see tip, page 57)
1	cup chopped onions
1	fresh jalapeño pepper, seeded and chopped (see tip, page 57)
4½	teaspoons minced fresh garlic
4½	teaspoons sugar
1	tablespoon kosher salt
6	dried ancho chile peppers, seeded and cut into 1-inch pieces
1½	teaspoons lime juice
¼	cup white vinegar

1 Preheat broiler. Place tomatoes in a single layer in a 15×10×1-inch baking pan. Broil 3 to 4 inches from the heat for 8 to 10 minutes, turning once, until skins are lightly charred. Transfer to a cutting board. When cool enough to handle, remove and discard loose skins,* coarsely chop, and transfer to a large stainless-steel, enameled, or nonstick pot.

2 Meanwhile, place the cumin seeds in a small skillet. Cook over medium heat, stirring frequently, until seeds are lightly toasted and fragrant. Remove from heat and let cool. Finely grind the seeds in a spice grinder or using a mortar and pestle; stir into the tomatoes in pot.

3 Add the poblano peppers, onions, jalapeño peppers, garlic, sugar, and salt to the tomato mixture. Bring to boiling, stirring frequently. Reduce heat and simmer, uncovered, until peppers and onions are soft, about 30 minutes. Stir in ancho chiles. Cover and let stand for 30 minutes.

4 Working in batches, transfer tomato mixture to a food processor or blender. Cover and process or blend until smooth. Strain mixture through a fine-mesh sieve, pushing liquid through and scraping the inside of the sieve using a rubber spatula; discard solids. Repeat with remaining mixture. Return strained mixture to the large pot. Bring to boiling; reduce heat. Simmer sauce, uncovered, about 10 minutes or until slightly thickened and reduced to about 4 cups. Stir in lime juice and vinegar.

5 Ladle hot sauce into hot, sterilized half-pint jars, leaving a ¼-inch headspace. Wipe jar rims; adjust lids.

6 Process filled jars in a boiling-water canner for 35 minutes (start timing when water returns to boiling). Remove jars from canner; cool on wire racks. **Makes 5 half-pints.**

PER ¼ CUP: 32 cal., 0 g fat, 0 mg chol., 301 mg sodium, 7 g carbo., 1 g fiber, 1 g pro.

*TEST KITCHEN TIP: You do not need to remove all of the skins because the sauce will be strained later.

Green Tomato-Pineapple Chutney

This sweet and hot Thai-style condiment is delicious with grilled fish or chicken.

PREP: 30 minutes   **COOK:** 1 hour   **PROCESS:** 10 minutes

3   pounds green tomatoes, cored and chopped into ¾-inch pieces (about 8 cups)
2   cups chopped fresh pineapple
4   cups sugar
1   cup water
2   tablespoons grated fresh ginger
1   teaspoon finely shredded lime peel
2   tablespoons lime juice
1   tablespoon finely chopped fresh garlic
1   cup lightly packed fresh cilantro leaves, snipped
½   cup lightly packed fresh mint leaves, snipped
1   to 2 fresh Thai chiles, finely chopped (see tip, page 57)

1 In a 4- to 6-quart stainless-steel, enamel, or nonstick heavy pot combine green tomatoes, pineapple, sugar, water, ginger, lime peel, lime juice, and garlic. Bring to boiling, stirring frequently until sugar dissolves. Reduce heat and simmer, uncovered, about 1 hour or until mixture is thickened. Stir in cilantro, mint, and Thai chiles.

2 Ladle into hot, sterilized half-pint canning jars, leaving a ¼-inch headspace. Wipe jar rims; adjust lids.

3 Process in a boiling-water canner for 10 minutes (start timing when water returns to boiling). Remove jars from canner; cool on wire racks. **Makes 5 half-pints.**

PER 2 TABLESPOONS: 92 cal., 0 g fat, 0 mg chol., 6 mg sodium, 23 g carb., 1 g dietary fiber, 22 g sugar, 1 g protein.

To cut up a fresh pineapple, first cut off the crown and a thin slice off the bottom. Place the pineapple upright on a cutting board. With a sharp knife, cut down the sides of the fruit to remove the tough outer skin. Cut the pineapple in 8 wedges, then use the knife to cut the core, end to end, out of each wedge.

Balsamic Cherry Tomato-Caramelized Onion Conserve

Top a wheel of Brie with this sweet-savory melange before warming it in the oven and serving it with slices of toasted baguette—or use it as a bruschetta or crostini topping.

PREP: 30 minutes **COOK:** 16 to 20 minutes **PROCESS:** 5 minutes

2	tablespoons butter
2	tablespoons olive oil
2	pounds sweet onions (such as Vidalia or Walla Walla), quartered and thinly sliced
2	teaspoons sea salt
1	teaspoon sugar
2	pints cherry tomatoes, halved
¾	cup honey
¼	cup balsamic vinegar
½	teaspoon freshly ground black pepper

1 In a very large skillet heat butter and oil over medium-low heat until butter melts. Add onions, salt, and sugar. Cook, covered, for 13 to 15 minutes or until onions are tender, stirring occasionally. Uncover; cook and stir over medium-high heat for 3 to 5 minutes or until deep golden brown.

2 Stir the cherry tomatoes and honey into the onion mixture. Bring to boiling over high heat. Reduce heat to medium-high and boil for 5 minutes or until tomatoes are just softened, stirring frequently. Remove from heat. Stir in balsamic vinegar and pepper.

3 Ladle hot mixture into hot, sterilized half-pint canning jars, leaving a ¼-inch headspace. Wipe jar rims; adjust lids.

4 Process filled jars in a boiling-water canner for 5 minutes (start timing when water returns to boiling). Remove jars from canner; cool on wire racks. **Makes about 5 half-pints.**

PER 2 TABLESPOONS: 42 cal., 1 g fat (0 g sat. fat), 2 mg chol., 147 mg sodium, 8 g carbo., 0 g fiber, 0 g pro.

TEST KITCHEN tip

Don't try to speed up the cooking time for the onions by turning up the heat. The key to the supersweet flavor and melt-in-your mouth buttery texture of caramelized onions is fairly long cooking over medium-low heat.

Can It!

CHAPTER 4

Scent of Citrus

It's irresistibly easy to transform citrus fruit into a marmalade, curd, or jelly. The result is a taste of sunshine in a jar ready to enjoy year-round.

Lemon-Honey Jelly

The flower nectar used to make a honey determines the honey's taste, so you can change the flavor of this jelly by the honey you choose. Clover honey provides the mildest flavor, while buckwheat or blackberry honey provides a more pronounced flavor.

PREP: 45 minutes   **PROCESS:** 5 minutes

2	to 3 medium lemons
1½	cups water
3½	cups sugar
¾	cup honey
½	of a 6-ounce package (1 foil pouch) liquid fruit pectin

1. Using a vegetable peeler, remove the colored part of the peel from one of the lemons. (Avoid removing the white portion.) Cut the peel into thin strips; set aside. Cut the remaining lemons in half; squeeze lemons for juice. Measure ½ cup lemon juice. (Reserve any remaining juice for another use.)

2. In a 5- to 6-quart heavy pot combine lemon peel strips, the ½ cup lemon juice, and water. Add sugar. Cook and stir over medium heat until the sugar dissolves. Stir in honey. Bring to a full rolling boil, stirring constantly. Quickly stir in the pectin. Return to a full rolling boil, stirring constantly. Boil hard for 1 minute, stirring constantly. Remove from heat. Quickly skim off the foam with a metal spoon. Use spoon to remove the lemon peel strips; discard peel strips.

3. Ladle hot jelly into hot, sterilized half-pint canning jars, leaving a ¼-inch headspace. Wipe jar rims; adjust lids.

4. Process filled jars in a boiling-water canner for 5 minutes (start timing when water returns to boiling). Remove jars from canner; cool on wire racks. **Makes 5 half-pints.**

PER TABLESPOON: 44 cal., 0 g fat, 0 mg chol., 0 mg sodium, 12 g carbo., 0 g fiber, 0 g pro.

TEST KITCHEN tip

Ranging in size from that of a large egg to an orange, lemons are available year-round. However, they are their tastiest during the summer months, from June until August.

Grapefruit Curd

This is delicious spread on toast—or spooned into tiny tart shells for a quick dessert.

PREP: 20 minutes   **CHILL:** 1 hour

1   cup sugar
2   tablespoons cornstarch
1   teaspoon finely shredded
     grapefruit peel (set aside)
½   cup grapefruit juice
¼   cup water
6   egg yolks, lightly beaten
½   cup butter, cut up

1 In a medium saucepan stir together sugar and cornstarch. Stir in grapefruit juice and the water. Cook and stir over medium heat until thickened and bubbly.

2 Stir half of the grapefruit mixture into the egg yolks. Return yolk mixture to the saucepan. Cook, stirring constantly, over medium heat until mixture comes to a gentle boil. Cook and stir for 2 minutes more. Remove from heat. Add butter pieces, stirring until melted. Stir in grapefruit peel. Cover surface with plastic wrap. Chill for at least 1 hour before serving. Store curd in the refrigerator for up to 1 week or transfer curd to a freezer container and freeze for up to 2 months. **Makes 2 cups.**

PER TABLESPOON: 63 cal., 4 g fat (2 g sat. fat), 50 mg chol., 22 mg sodium, 7 g carbo., 0 g fiber, 1 g pro.

Tangerine Marmalade

Tangerines enjoy peak season from late October to April but are especially abundant during the winter.

PREP: 35 minutes **PROCESS:** 5 minutes **STAND:** 2 weeks

10	**to 12 medium tangerines**
7	**cups sugar**
½	**of a 6-ounce package (1 foil pouch) liquid fruit pectin**

1 Peel tangerines, reserving peels. Section tangerines, reserving juices; discard sectioned membranes. Chop fruit; reserve juices and discard seeds. (You should have 3 cups fruit and ¾ cup juice.) Using a sharp knife, scrape off the white portions of peels; discard. Cut enough of the peels into very thin strips to measure ¾ cup.

2 In an 8- to 10-quart pot combine chopped fruit, reserved juices, peel strips, and sugar. Bring to a full rolling boil. Stir in pectin; return to a full boil. Boil hard for 1 minute, stirring constantly. Remove from heat. Quickly skim off foam with a metal spoon.

3 Ladle hot marmalade into hot, sterilized half-pint or 4-ounce canning jars, leaving a ½-inch headspace. Wipe jar rims; adjust lids.

4 Process filled jars in a boiling-water canner for 5 minutes (start timing when water returns to boiling). Remove jars from canner; cool on wire racks. To distribute fruit, cool about 20 minutes, then gently turn and tilt jars without inverting them; repeat as needed. Let set at room temperature for 2 weeks before serving. **Makes 7 half-pints or fourteen 4-ounce jars.**

PER TABLESPOON: 53 cal., 0 g fat, 0 mg chol., 0 mg sodium, 14 g carbo., 0 g fiber, 0 g pro.

Blood Orange and Beaujolais Marmalade

This deep red marmalade makes a luscious glaze for roast pork. Or just spoon it over shortbread cookies for an afternoon treat with tea.

PREP: 45 minutes   **COOK:** 30 minutes   **PROCESS:** 5 minutes   **STAND:** 2 weeks

4   **medium blood oranges or oranges**
1   **medium lemon**
1   **cup Beaujolais wine or other medium-bodied red wine**
½   **cup water**
⅛   **teaspoon baking soda**
5   **cups sugar**
½   **of a 6-ounce package (1 foil pouch) liquid fruit pectin**

1 Score the peel of each blood orange and the lemon into four lengthwise sections; remove peels with your fingers. Using a sharp knife, scrape off the white portions of peels; discard. Cut peels into thin strips and coarsely chop. In a medium saucepan combine chopped peels, wine, the water, and baking soda. Bring to boiling; reduce heat. Simmer, covered, for 20 minutes. Do not drain.

2 Section blood oranges and lemon, reserving juices. Add fruit and juices to peel mixture; return to boiling. Simmer, covered, for 10 minutes.

3 In an 8- to 10-quart heavy pot combine fruit mixture and sugar. Bring to a full rolling boil, stirring constantly. Quickly stir in pectin. Return to a full rolling boil; boil for 1 minute, stirring constantly. Remove from heat; skim off foam with a metal spoon.

4 Ladle hot marmalade into hot, sterilized half-pint canning jars, leaving a ¼-inch headspace. Wipe jar rims; adjust lids. Process filled jars in a boiling-water canner for 5 minutes (start timing when water returns to boiling). Remove jars; cool on racks. To distribute fruit, cool for about 20 minutes, then gently turn and tilt jars without inverting them; repeat as needed. Let marmalade set for 2 weeks before serving. **Makes 4 half-pints.**

PER TABLESPOON: 68 cal., 0 g fat, 0 mg chol., 3 mg sodium, 17 g carbo., 0 g fiber, 0 g pro.

Preserved Orange Slices

These flavor-packed treats make a festive between-meal snack during the holidays.

PREP: 35 minutes   **COOK:** 1 hour 45 minutes   **PROCESS:** 10 minutes

8	**medium seedless oranges**
4	**cups sugar**
1	**cup white vinegar**
½	**cup water**
6	**whole cloves**
6	**whole allspice**
2	**3-inch cinnamon sticks, broken**

1 Cut off and discard enough of the top and bottom of each orange to expose the flesh. Cut the oranges in half lengthwise; cut crosswise into ¼-inch-thick slices. Place the orange slices in a 4-quart stainless-steel, enamel, or nonstick heavy pot; add enough water to cover orange slices. Bring to boiling over medium-high heat, stirring occasionally. Reduce heat to low. Cover and simmer for about 45 minutes or until the oranges are tender, stirring occasionally. Drain well.

2 Return drained oranges to the pot. Add sugar, vinegar, and the ½ cup water. For a spice bag, cut a 6- to 8-inch square from a double thickness of 100%-cotton cheesecloth. Place cloves, allspice, and cinnamon sticks in center of cheesecloth square. Bring up the corners; tie closed with 100%-cotton kitchen string. Add spice bag to the pot. Bring to boiling over medium-high heat, stirring constantly until sugar dissolves. Reduce heat to low. Simmer, uncovered, for about 1 hour or until oranges are well glazed.

3 Remove and discard spice bag. Using a slotted spoon, remove orange slices from the syrup and pack them into hot, sterilized half-pint canning jars. Ladle the hot syrup over the orange slices, leaving a ¼-inch headspace. Wipe jar rims; adjust lids.

4 Process filled jars in a boiling-water canner for 10 minutes (start timing when water returns to boiling). Remove jars from canner; cool on wire racks. **Makes 6 half-pints.**

PER 2 TABLESPOONS: 76 cal., 0 g fat, 0 mg chol., 0 mg sodium, 19 g carbo., 1 g fiber, 0 g pro.

Meyer Lemon and Rosemary Marmalade

Meyer lemons are a cross between a lemon and an orange. Their flesh is slightly sweeter and less acidic than that of regular lemons. Serve this spread with everything from biscuits to dinner rolls to bagels.

PREP: 40 minutes   **COOK:** 30 minutes   **PROCESS:** 5 minutes

1½   pounds Meyer lemons
    (about 6 medium)
1½   cups water
2   tablespoons snipped fresh
    rosemary
⅛   teaspoon baking soda
5   cups sugar
½   of a 6-ounce package (1 foil
    pouch) liquid fruit pectin

1 Score the peel of each lemon into four lengthwise sections; remove the peels with your fingers. Using a sharp knife, scrape off and discard the white portions of peels. Cut peels into thin strips. Measure about 1½ cups peel strips.

2 In a medium saucepan bring the 1½ cups lemon peel strips, the water, rosemary, and baking soda to boiling; reduce heat. Simmer, covered, for 20 minutes. Do not drain.

3 Section lemons, reserving juices; discard seeds. Add lemon sections and reserved juice to peels. Return to boiling; reduce heat. Simmer, covered, for 10 minutes. Measure about 2½ cups lemon mixture.

4 In a 6- to 8-quart heavy pot combine the 2½ cups simmered lemon mixture and sugar. Bring to full rolling boil, stirring constantly until sugar dissolves. Quickly stir in pectin. Return to full rolling boil, stirring constantly. Boil hard for 1 minute, stirring constantly. Remove from heat. Skim off foam with a metal spoon, being careful not to remove peel.

5 Ladle hot marmalade into hot, sterilized half-pint canning jars, leaving a ¼-inch headspace. Wipe jar rims; adjust lids.

6 Process filled jars in a boiling-water canner for 5 minutes (start timing when water returns to boiling). Remove jars from canner; cool on wire racks for 20 minutes. To distribute fruit, gently turn and tilt jars; repeat cooling and tilting as needed. (Do not invert the sealed jars.) **Makes 5 half-pints**.

PER TABLESPOON: 51 cal., 0 gl fat, 0 mg chol., 2 mg sodium, 14 g carbo., 0 g fiber, 0 g pro.

Can It!

CHAPTER 5

Happy Couples

When two meant to be ingredients join together in perfect harmony, the results are pure, soulful scrumptiousness. These exquisite marriages of flavor are sure to please.

Berry-Rhubarb Salsa

Brighten this salsa by stirring ⅓ cup chopped fresh strawberries and 1 tablespoon chopped fresh mint into each half-pint at serving time.

PREP: 25 minutes   **PROCESS:** 15 minutes

2	pounds rhubarb, cut into 1-inch pieces (6 cups)
1½	cups sugar
1½	cups dried cranberries
¾	cup cider vinegar
1	tablespoon grated fresh ginger
2	cups coarsely chopped strawberries

1 In a large stainless-steel, enamel, or nonstick heavy saucepan combine rhubarb, sugar, cranberries, vinegar, and ginger. Bring to boiling, stirring occasionally; reduce heat. Simmer, uncovered, for 5 minutes. Remove from heat. Stir in berries.

2 Ladle into hot, sterilized half-pint canning jars, leaving a ½-inch headspace. Wipe jar rims; adjust lids.

3 Process filled jars in a boiling-water canner for 15 minutes (start timing when water returns to boiling). Remove jars from canner; cool on wire racks. **Makes 6 half-pints.**

PER TABLESPOON: 21 cal., 0 g fat, 0 mg chol., 1 mg sodium, 5 g carbo., 0 g fiber, 0 g pro.

Blueberry-Cinnamon Freezer Jam

Double the cinnamon flavor by serving this spiced berry jam with toasted cinnamon-raisin bread.

PREP: 20 minutes   **STAND:** 10 minutes + 24 hours

5¼	**cups sugar**
3	**cups crushed blueberries**
1	**teaspoon ground cinnamon**
1	**1.75-ounce package regular powdered fruit pectin**
¾	**cup water**

1 In a large bowl combine sugar, blueberries, and cinnamon. Let stand at room temperature for 10 minutes, stirring occasionally.

2 In a small saucepan stir pectin into the water. Bring to boiling, stirring constantly. Boil hard for 1 minute, stirring constantly. Remove from heat. Add to blueberry mixture; stir for about 3 minutes or until sugar dissolves and mixture is not grainy.

3 Ladle jam into half-pint freezer containers, leaving a ½-inch headspace. Seal and label. Let stand at room temperature for 24 hours before storing. Store for up to 3 weeks in the refrigerator or for up to 1 year in the freezer. **Makes 4 half-pints.**

PER TABLESPOON: 70 cal., 0 g fat, 0 mg chol., 1 mg sodium, 18 g carbo., 0 g fiber, 0 g pro.

Rhubarb and Rose Petal Jam

Tart but tasty rhubarb and the crisp floral flavor of rose petals create a match made in heaven. For a special treat, serve the jam with tea biscuits and rose hip tea.

PREP: 45 minutes   **STAND:** 30 minutes   **PROCESS:** 10 minutes

6½   **cups sugar**
1   **cup water**
4   **ounces pink or red edible rose petals (6 cups)**
2½   **pounds fresh rhubarb**
1   **1.75-ounce package regular powdered fruit pectin**

1 For syrup, in a stainless-steel, enamel, or nonstick 4-quart Dutch oven combine 1 cup of the sugar and the water. Cook and stir until sugar dissolves. Bring mixture to boiling. Stir in rose petals. Remove from heat. Using the back of a wooden spoon, slightly mash rose petals. Cover and let stand for 30 minutes. Strain mixture through a fine-mesh sieve set over a large bowl. Discard petals.

2 Meanwhile, finely chop rhubarb. In the same Dutch oven combine rhubarb and the strained syrup. Bring to boiling over high heat. Reduce heat and simmer for about 2 minutes or until rhubarb is tender. Measure 4½ cups of the rhubarb mixture and return to Dutch oven. Stir pectin into rhubarb mixture. Bring to a full rolling boil over high heat, stirring constantly. Stir in the remaining 5½ cups sugar. Return to a full rolling boil, stirring constantly. Boil hard for 1 minute, stirring constantly. Remove from heat. Skim off foam with a metal spoon.

3 Ladle hot jam into hot, sterilized half-pint canning jars, leaving a ¼-inch headspace. Wipe jar rims; adjust lids.

4 Process filled jars in a boiling-water canner for 10 minutes (start timing when water returns to boiling). Remove jars from canner; cool on wire racks. **Makes 7 half-pints.**

PER TABLESPOON: 48 cal., 0 g fat, 0 mg chol., 1 mg sodium, 12 g carbo., 0 g fiber, 0 g pro.

White Chocolate and Raspberry Spread

Tartly sweet raspberries mesh magnificently with creamy white chocolate. Sandwich the spread between cookies or pound cake slices.

PREP: 35 minutes   **PROCESS:** 10 minutes

6   **cups raspberries**
1   **vanilla bean, split lengthwise**
1   **1.75-ounce package regular powdered fruit pectin**
6   **cups sugar**
9   **ounces white baking chocolate (with cocoa butter), finely chopped**
2   **teaspoons vanilla extract**

1 In a 4- to 6-quart heavy pot use a potato masher to slightly crush raspberries. Add vanilla bean. Heat raspberry mixture over medium heat for 5 minutes, stirring occasionally. Slowly add the pectin, stirring constantly. Bring mixture to a full rolling boil, stirring constantly. Add sugar. Return to a full rolling boil, stirring constantly. Boil hard for 1 minute, stirring constantly.

2 Remove from heat. Discard vanilla bean. Add white chocolate, stirring until chocolate is completely melted. Stir in vanilla extract.

3 Ladle hot spread into hot, sterilized half-pint canning jars, leaving a ¼-inch headspace. Wipe jar rims; adjust lids.

4 Process filled jars in a boiling-water canner for 10 minutes (start timing when water returns to boiling). Remove jars from canner; cool on wire racks. **Makes 8 half-pints.**

PER TABLESPOON: 52 cal., 1 g fat (0 g sat. fat), 0 mg chol., 3 mg sodium, 12 g carbo., 0 g fiber, 0 g pro.

TEST KITCHEN tip

Raspberries come in a variety of colors:

RED These are great for munching right off the plant, but they also are ideal for cooking and preserving.
YELLOW Sweeter and less acidic than other raspberries, yellow raspberries are best for eating out of hand.

BLACK Smaller and seedier than other raspberries, these intensely sweet berries work well in jellies and other strained concoctions.
PURPLE A cross between red and black raspberries, purple raspberries possess excellent flavor and preserve well.

Raspberry-Orange Freezer Jam

Freezer jams like this one are terrific recipes if you're new to canning and preserving. They are truly easy—just mix the fruit and other ingredients, cook it a little bit, divide, and freeze.

PREP: 20 minutes   **STAND:** 10 minutes + 24 hours

5½ cups sugar
3 cups crushed raspberries
½ teaspoon finely shredded orange peel
1 1.75-ounce package regular powdered fruit pectin
¾ cup water

1 In a large bowl combine sugar, raspberries, and orange peel. Let stand at room temperature for 10 minutes, stirring occasionally.

2 In a small saucepan stir pectin into the water. Bring to boiling, stirring constantly. Boil hard for 1 minute, stirring constantly. Remove from heat. Add to raspberry mixture; stir about 3 minutes or until sugar dissolves and mixture is not grainy.

3 Ladle jam into half-pint freezer containers, leaving a ½-inch head space. Seal and label. Let stand at room temperature for 24 hours before storing. Store for up to 3 weeks in the refrigerator or for up to 1 year in the freezer. **Makes 4 half-pints.**

PER TABLESPOON: 73 cal., 0 g fat, 0 mg chol., 1 mg sodium, 19 g carbo., 0 g fiber, 0 g pro.

Be sure to just get the orange part of the skin when you're shredding the orange peel. It contains the aromatic oils that infuse this jam with flavor. The white layer underneath, called the pith, is bitter.

Very Berry-Rhubarb Jam

This easy-to-make jam makes a tasty topping on warm biscuits. Make it in the spring, when fresh rhubarb is at its plentiful peak.

PREP: 30 minutes   **STAND:** 8 hours

2   **pounds rhubarb, cut into 1-inch pieces (6 cups)**
5   **cups sugar**
¾   **cup water**
1   **21-ounce can blueberry pie filling**
2   **3-ounce packages raspberry-flavor gelatin**

1 In a 4- to 6-quart heavy pot combine rhubarb, sugar, and the water. Bring to boiling; reduce heat. Simmer, uncovered, for 5 minutes, stirring constantly.

2 Stir in blueberry pie filling. Return to boiling; boil for 6 minutes, stirring constantly. Stir in gelatin. Return to boiling; boil for 3 minutes, stirring constantly.

3 Ladle hot jam into half-pint freezer containers, leaving a ½-inch headspace. Seal and label. Let stand at room temperature for about 8 hours or until jam is set. Store for up to 3 weeks in the refrigerator or for up to 1 year in the freezer. **Makes 8 half-pints.**

PER TABLESPOON: 45 cal., 0 g fat, 0 mg chol., 6 mg sodium, 11 g carbo., 0 g fiber, 0 g pro.

TEST KITCHEN tip

If the strings on your rhubarb are too fibrous and thick, you can remove them. At one end of the stalk, cut just under the skin. Pull the piece down to remove the strings. Continue until all of the strings are off, then slice the rhubarb.

Can It!

Cider 'n' Spice Jelly

This tried-and-true flavor pairing tastes fantastic on toasted bagels and fresh biscuits. When warmed, it also makes a great glaze on pound cake.

PREP: 35 minutes **COOK:** 21 minutes **PROCESS:** 5 minutes

5   cups fresh-pressed
     apple cider
2   3-inch cinnamon
     sticks, broken
8   whole allspice
8   whole cloves
7½   cups sugar
½   of a 6-ounce package
     (1 foil pouch) liquid
     fruit pectin

1 In a 6- to 8-quart stainless-steel, enamel, or nonstick heavy pot combine cider, cinnamon, allspice, and cloves. Cover and bring to boiling; reduce heat to medium-low. Simmer, covered, for 20 minutes. Line a sieve with a double layer of 100%-cotton cheesecloth; set sieve over a large bowl. Strain cider mixture through sieve. If desired, reserve the spices to add to canning jars.

2 Wash the pot, then return strained cider to the pot. Add sugar; stir to combine. Bring to a full rolling boil, stirring constantly. Add pectin. Return to a full rolling boil, stirring constantly. Boil hard for 1 minute, stirring constantly. Remove from heat.

3 Ladle hot jelly into hot, sterilized half-pint canning jars, leaving a ¼-inch headspace. If desired, add some of the reserved cinnamon, allspice, and cloves to each jar. Wipe jar rims; adjust lids.

4 Process filled jars in a boiling-water canner for 5 minutes (start timing when water returns to boiling). Remove jars from canner; cool on wire racks. **Makes 7 half-pints.**

PER TABLESPOON: 57 cal., 0 g fat, 0 mg chol., 0 mg sodium, 14 g carbo., 0 g fiber, 0 g pro.

Cranberry-Tangerine Spread

For an irresistible party treat, spoon some of this cinnamon-spiced fruit spread over a softened block of cream cheese and serve it alongside water crackers.

PREP: 20 minutes   **COOK:** 30 minutes   **COOL:** 1 hour   **PROCESS:** 5 minutes

1   **12-ounce package cranberries**
1   **cup water**
½   **cup tangerine juice or orange juice**
3   **cups sugar**
2½   **inches stick cinnamon**

1 In a large heavy saucepan combine cranberries, the water, and tangerine juice. Bring to boiling; reduce heat. Simmer, covered, for about 5 minutes or until cranberries pop. Remove from heat; cool for 1 hour.

2 Transfer cranberry mixture to a blender or food processor. Cover and blend or process until smooth; return to saucepan. Stir in sugar and cinnamon. Bring to boiling, stirring constantly; reduce heat. Simmer, uncovered, for about 25 minutes or until mixture is thickened, stirring frequently. Remove from heat. Remove and discard cinnamon stick.

3 Ladle hot spread into hot, sterilized 4-ounce canning jars, leaving a ¼-inch headspace. Wipe jar rims; adjust lids.

4 Process filled jars in a boiling-water canner for 5 minutes (start timing when water returns to boiling). Remove jars from canner; cool on wire racks. **Makes six 4-ounce jars.**

PER TABLESPOON: 53 cal., 0 g fat, 0 mg chol., 0 mg sodium, 14 g carbo., 0 g fiber, 0 g pro.

TEST KITCHEN *tip*

Tangerines come in several varieties. Honey tangerines are a cross between a tangerine and an orange. Fairchild tangerines are juicy and rich tasting but can be a little tough to peel. And Minneola tangerines, or tangelos, are a tangerine-grapefruit cross with a mellow and sweet flavor. You can use any type in this recipe.

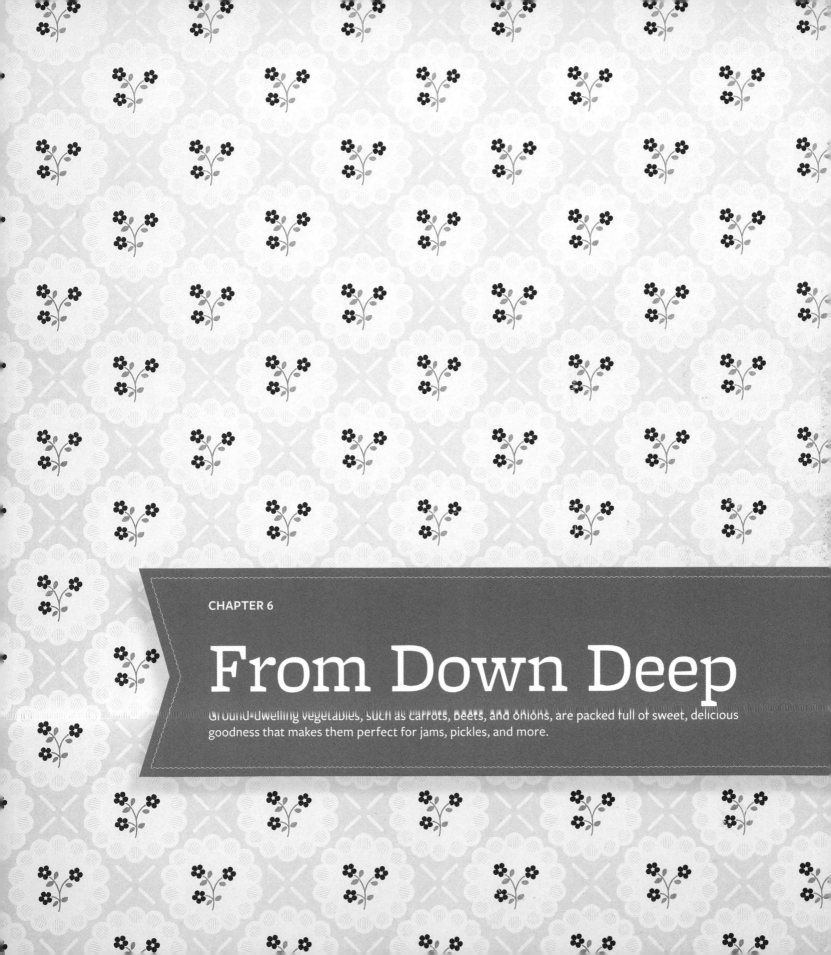

CHAPTER 6

From Down Deep

Ground-dwelling vegetables, such as carrots, beets, and onions, are packed full of sweet, delicious goodness that makes them perfect for jams, pickles, and more.

Carrot Cake Jam

Slather this jam onto pieces of toast with a little cream cheese and your breakfast will taste like dessert.

PREP: 25 minutes **COOK:** 21 minutes **PROCESS:** 10 minutes

2	cups finely shredded carrots (4 medium)
1	cup finely chopped, peeled pear (1 medium)
1	15-ounce can crushed pineapple (juice pack), undrained
2	tablespoons lemon juice
1	teaspoon ground cinnamon
½	teaspoon ground nutmeg
1	1.75-ounce package regular powdered fruit pectin
4	cups granulated sugar
2	cups packed brown sugar
¼	cup flaked coconut or raisins (optional)
1	teaspoon vanilla

1. In a 4- to 6-quart heavy pot combine carrots, pear, pineapple with the juice, lemon juice, cinnamon, and nutmeg. Bring to boiling, stirring constantly; reduce heat. Simmer, covered, for 20 minutes, stirring frequently. Remove from heat. Sprinkle mixture with pectin; stir until pectin dissolves.

2. Bring carrot mixture to boiling, stirring constantly. Add granulated sugar and brown sugar. Return to a full rolling boil; boil for 1 minute, stirring constantly. Remove from heat. Quickly skim off foam with a metal spoon. Stir in coconut or raisins (if desired) and vanilla.

3. Ladle hot jam into hot, sterilized half-pint canning jars, leaving a ¼-inch headspace. Wipe jar rims; adjust lids.

4. Process filled jars in a boiling-water canner for 10 minutes (start timing when water returns to boiling). Remove jars from canner; cool on wire racks. **Makes 7 half-pints.**

PER TABLESPOON: 48 cal., 0 g fat, 0 mg chol., 3 mg sodium, 13 g carbo., 0 g fiber, 0 g pro.

TEST KITCHEN *tip*

Save yourself some work! Young, tender carrots seldom need peeling. Just give them a good scrub with a stiff brush.

Asian Pickled Carrots

Serve these crunchy orange veggies as an appetizer before an Asian-inspired dinner.

START TO FINISH: 55 minutes

1 **pound carrots, bias-sliced into ¾-inch pieces (halve any thick carrots lengthwise)**
1 **teaspoon salt**
¼ **cup thin strips of peeled fresh ginger**
3 **whole allspice**
¾ **cup water**
¾ **cup rice vinegar**
⅓ **cup packed brown sugar**
4 **whole cloves**
4 **whole black peppercorns**

1 In a covered large saucepan cook carrots with salt in a small amount of boiling water for about 3 minutes or until crisp-tender; drain.

2 Pack carrots into three sterilized half-pint canning jars or other jars. Divide fresh ginger among jars; place one of the whole allspice in each jar.

3 In a small stainless-steel, enamel, or nonstick heavy saucepan combine the water, vinegar, brown sugar, cloves, and peppercorns. Bring to boiling; reduce heat. Simmer, uncovered, for 5 minutes.

4 Pour hot vinegar mixture over carrots. Wipe jar rims; adjust lids. Cool. Seal and label. Store in the refrigerator for up to 3 months. **Makes 3 half-pints.**

PER ⅓ CUP: 18 cal., 0 g fat, 0 mg chol., 135 mg sodium, 5 g carbo., 1 g fiber, 0 g pro.

TEST KITCHEN tip

Use a vegetable peeler or a paring knife to remove the tough brown outer skin of fresh gingerroot before cutting it into thin strips for this recipe.

Pickled Beets

Top a bed of vinaigrette-dressed greens with these perfectly spiced beets and sprinkle with crumbled blue cheese and toasted walnuts for an elegant winter salad.

PREP: 20 minutes   **COOK:** 30 minutes   **PROCESS:** 30 minutes

3   pounds small (2-inch-diameter) whole beets
2   cups vinegar
1   cup water
½   cup sugar
1   teaspoon whole allspice
6   whole cloves
3   inches stick cinnamon

1 Wash beets. Cut off beet tops, leaving 1 inch of stems; trim root ends. Do not peel. In a large saucepan cook beets, covered, in boiling, lightly salted water for about 25 minutes or until tender; drain. Cool beets slightly; trim off roots and stems. Slip off and discard the skins. Quarter beets.

2 For pickling liquid, in a medium stainless-steel, enamel, or nonstick heavy saucepan combine vinegar, the water, and sugar. Place allspice, cloves, and cinnamon in the center of a double-thick, 6-inch square of 100%-cotton cheesecloth. Bring up corners; tie closed with clean kitchen string. Add spice bag to saucepan. Bring to boiling; reduce heat. Simmer, uncovered, for 5 minutes. Remove and discard spice bag.

3 Pack beets into hot, sterilized half-pint canning jars, leaving a ½-inch headspace. Pour hot pickling liquid over beets, maintaining the ½-inch headspace. Wipe jar rims; adjust lids.

4 Process filled jars in a boiling-water canner for 30 minutes (start timing when water returns to boiling). Remove jars from canner; cool on wire racks. **Makes 6 half-pints.**

PER ⅓ CUP: 29 cal., 0 g fat, 0 mg chol., 17 mg sodium, 8 g carbo., 1 g fiber, 0 g pro.

Although this recipe calls for small whole beets, you can use larger ones. Follow the directions, then after cooking and removing skins, cut the beets into 1-inch chunks or ¼-inch slices.

Pickled Beet and Sage Conserve

Many kinds of cheeses and roasted meats taste delicious with this conserve. Try it with slices of creamy Havarti or Danish blue cheese—or slices of crisp-skinned roast pork.

PREP: 20 minutes   **COOK:** 40 minutes

2   **16-ounce jars sliced or whole pickled beets**
2   **medium pears, cored, peeled, and coarsely chopped**
½   **cup sugar**
2   **tablespoons lemon juice**
1   **cup chopped walnuts, toasted**
2   **tablespoons snipped fresh sage**

1 Drain beets, reserving liquid from one of the jars (you should have ¾ cup liquid). Coarsely chop beets. In a large saucepan combine beets, pears, and the reserved liquid. Bring to boiling; reduce heat. Simmer, uncovered, for about 10 minutes or until pears are soft, stirring occasionally.

2 Stir sugar and lemon juice into beet mixture, stirring until sugar dissolves. Bring to boiling; reduce heat. Simmer, uncovered, for about 30 minutes or until mixture is thickened, stirring often. Remove from heat. Stir in walnuts and sage. Cool.

3 Transfer conserve to a sterilized jar or an airtight container. Seal and label. Store in the refrigerator for up to 2 days or transfer to a freezer container and freeze for up to 3 months. **Makes 4 cups.**

PER 2 TABLESPOONS: 61 cal., 2 g fat (0 g sat. fat), 0 mg chol., 75 mg sodium, 10 g carbo., 1 g fiber, 1 g pro.

Beets reach their best canning potential in midsummer, when they are small and tender and before they have grown tough and woody.

Vidalia Onion and Maple Conserve

For an incredible appetizer, top baked squares of puff pastry with this savory-sweet conserve, goat cheese, and fresh thyme. For a more intense flavor, use aged sherry vinegar in the conserve.

PREP: 30 minutes   **COOK:** 30 minutes   **PROCESS:** 5 minutes

¼   cup butter
¼   cup olive oil
2½ pounds Vidalia onions or other sweet onions (such as Walla Walla or Maui), quartered
2   teaspoons sea salt
2   tablespoons fresh thyme leaves
1   teaspoon freshly ground black pepper
1   cup pure maple syrup
¼   cup sherry vinegar

1 In an extra-large skillet heat butter and oil over medium-high heat until butter melts. Add onions and salt. Cook for about 5 minutes or until onions start to soften, stirring frequently. Reduce heat to medium-low; add thyme and pepper. Cover skillet; cook for 10 to 12 minutes or until onions are very tender, stirring twice.

2 Increase heat to medium-high. Add maple syrup; bring just to boiling. Reduce heat to medium. Cook, uncovered, for 15 to 20 minutes or until most of the liquid has evaporated, stirring frequently. Remove from heat; stir in vinegar.

3 Ladle hot mixture into hot, sterilized 4-ounce canning jars, leaving a ¼-inch headspace. Wipe jar rims; adjust lids.

4 Process filled jars in a boiling-water canner for 5 minutes (start timing when water returns to boiling). Remove jars from canner; cool on wire racks. **Makes about 5 (4-ounce) jars.**

PER 2 TABLESPOONS: 109 cal., 5 g fat (2 g sat. fat), 6 mg chol., 180 mg sodium, 16 g carbo., 1 g fiber, 1 g pro.

TEST KITCHEN *tip*

Remove the aroma of onions from your hands by rubbing your fingers on a stainless-steel spoon.

Pepper and Honey Radish Pickles

These crunchy-sweet pink spheres are delicious on a tossed salad, as a condiment alongside a roast chicken, or simply as a stand-alone snack.

PREP: 40 minutes   **CHILL:** 1 to 2 hours   **COOK:** 15 minutes   **PROCESS:** 10 minutes

2	**pounds radishes, tops and roots removed**
2½	**cups water**
2	**tablespoons kosher salt**
1½	**cups water**
1¼	**cups white vinegar**
¾	**cup honey**
¼	**cup red wine vinegar**
2	**tablespoons mixed peppercorns**

1 Cut each radish into halves or quarters. In a large stainless-steel or glass bowl combine the 2½ cups water and the kosher salt. Add radishes. Cover and refrigerate for 1 to 2 hours. Drain and rinse radishes; set aside.

2 In a medium saucepan combine 1½ cups water, white vinegar, honey, red wine vinegar, and peppercorns. Bring to boiling, stirring occasionally. Reduce heat, cover, and simmer for 15 minutes.

3 Pack radishes into hot, sterilized half-pint jars, leaving a ¼-inch headspace. Ladle hot vinegar mixture into jars, being sure to get some peppercorns into each jar and maintaining the ¼-inch headspace. Discard any remaining vinegar mixture. Wipe jar rims; adjust lids.

4 Process filled jars in a boiling-water canner for 10 minutes (start timing when water returns to boiling). Remove jars from canner; cool on wire racks. **Makes 6 half-pints.**

PER ¼ CUP: 43 cal., 0 g fat, 0 mg chol., 509 mg sodium, 10 g carbo., 1 g fiber, 0 g pro.

TEST KITCHEN *tip*

Radishes are at their crispest—with the most peppery-sweet flavor—in spring. Radishes harvested in the summer heat are softer and less crunchy and can have a sharp, almost biting taste.

CHAPTER 7

Tropical Treasures

Fruits from the tropics flourish deliciously year-round—especially in the winter months. Their perpetual abundance allows passionate preservers to shine through all seasons.

Mango-Citrus Spread

This brightly flavored spread tastes amazing on warm corn bread—or try it as a glaze on grilled shrimp.

PREP: 30 minutes   **COOK:** 1 hour 5 minutes   **PROCESS:** 5 minutes

7	cups chopped mangoes
1	cup orange juice
¾	cup water
2½	cups sugar
2	teaspoons finely shredded lime peel
2	tablespoons lime juice

1 In a 4- to 6-quart stainless-steel, enamel, or nonstick heavy pot combine chopped mangoes, orange juice, and the water. Bring mixture to boiling over medium-high heat, stirring frequently. Reduce heat to low. Simmer, uncovered, about 30 minutes or until mangoes are very tender, stirring occasionally.

2 Place a food mill over a large bowl. Ladle cooked mango mixture into food mill; press the mixture into the bowl. (Or if you don't have a food mill, place a large sieve over a large bowl. Strain the mixture through the sieve, using the back of a spoon to press the mixture into the bowl.)

3 Return strained mango mixture to the large pot. Stir in sugar, lime peel, and lime juice. Bring to boiling over medium heat, stirring until sugar dissolves. Reduce heat to low. Simmer, uncovered, for 35 minutes. Remove from heat. Quickly skim off foam with a metal spoon.

4 Ladle hot mixture into hot, sterilized half-pint canning jars, leaving a ¼-inch headspace. Wipe jar rims; adjust lids.

5 Process filled jars in a boiling-water canner for 5 minutes (start timing when water returns to boiling). Remove jars from canner; cool on wire racks. **Makes 4 half-pints.**

PER TABLESPOON: 44 cal., 0 g fat, 0 mg chol., 0 mg sodium, 11 g carbo., 0 g fiber, 0 g pro.

Papaya-Rum Chutney

This chutney adds a tasty touch of sweetness to any sandwich. For a nonalcoholic version, omit the rum, but watch the mixture closely because the cooking time will be slightly less.

PREP: 40 minutes   **COOK:** 30 minutes   **PROCESS:** 10 minutes

5	to 6 papayas or 6 mangoes
4	large cloves garlic, quartered
4	large fresh chile peppers, such as poblano or jalapeño (see tip, page 57)
2	cups packed light brown sugar
1½	cups cider vinegar
½	cup light rum

1 Halve papayas; scoop out seeds. Peel and chop papayas. Measure 6 cups chopped fruit. (To prepare mangoes, make a cut through each mango, sliding a sharp knife next to one side of the seed. Repeat on other side of the seed, resulting in two large fruit pieces. Cut away all of the fruit that remains around the seed. Remove and discard peel on all pieces and chop the mango.) Place chopped fruit in a 4- to 6-quart stainless-steel, enamel, or nonstick heavy pot. Add garlic. Peel, seed, and chop chile peppers. Measure ½ cup chopped chile peppers; add to pot. Stir in brown sugar and vinegar.

2 Bring mixture to boiling over medium heat. Reduce heat. Stir in rum. Boil gently, uncovered, for 30 to 40 minutes or until mixture is desired consistency, stirring occasionally.

3 Ladle into hot, sterilized half-pint canning jars, leaving a ½-inch headspace. Wipe jar rims; adjust lids.

4 Process filled jars in a boiling-water canner for 10 minutes (start timing when water returns to boiling). Remove jars from canner; cool on wire racks. **Makes 5 half-pints.**

PER TABLESPOON: 36 cal., 0 g fat, 0 mg chol., 3 mg sodium, 8 g carbo., 0 g fiber, 0 g pro.

Tomato-Mango Chutney

This chutney makes a fabulous accompaniment to Jamaican jerk-spiced and grilled chicken skewers. Try it on a meaty grilled fish—such as halibut or sea bass—as well.

PREP: 30 minutes   **COOK:** 1 hour   **PROCESS:** 10 minutes

2	pounds tomatoes, peeled (if desired) and chopped (see tip, page 61)
2	medium mangoes, peeled, seeded, and chopped
4	teaspoons finely shredded lemon peel
2	teaspoons finely shredded lime peel
3½	cups granulated sugar
1¼	cups packed brown sugar
⅔	cup water

1 In a 4- to 6-quart stainless-steel, enamel, or nonstick heavy pot combine tomatoes, mangoes, lemon peel, and lime peel. Stir in granulated sugar, brown sugar, and the water. Bring to boiling; reduce heat. Simmer, uncovered, about 1 hour or until mixture sheets off a metal spoon.

2 Ladle into hot, sterilized half-pint canning jars, leaving a ¼-inch headspace. Wipe jar rims; adjust lids.

3 Process filled jars in a boiling-water canner for 10 minutes (start timing when water returns to boiling). Remove jars from canner; cool on wire racks. **Makes 5 half-pints.**

PER 2 TABLESPOONS: 105 cal., 0 g fat, 0 mg chol., 3 mg sodium, 27 g carbo., 0 g fiber, 0 g pro.

To prepare a mango, cut down through the fruit from top to bottom on both sides of the fruit. You will have two halves and the seed; discard the seed. Cut down through each half in strips the long way and then across to create chunks. Separate the chunks of fruit from the skin by sliding a sharp knife between the two.

Lime-Kiwi Freezer Jam

One spoonful of this bright green concoction proves that sweet kiwifruits and tart limes are a perfect match.

PREP: 35 minutes   **STAND:** 10 minutes + 24 hours   **COOL:** 15 minutes

2   cups mashed, peeled kiwifruits
(8 or 9 kiwifruits; about
1½ pounds)
4   cups sugar
1   teaspoon finely shredded
lime peel
½   cup water
¼   cup lime juice
1   1.75-ounce package regular
powdered fruit pectin

1 In a large bowl combine mashed kiwifruits, sugar, and lime peel. Let stand for 10 minutes, stirring occasionally. Meanwhile, in a small saucepan combine the water and lime juice. Stir in pectin. Bring to boiling over high heat. Boil hard for 1 minute, stirring constantly. Add pectin mixture to the fruit mixture, stirring about 3 minutes or until sugar dissolves and mixture is not grainy. Cool for 15 minutes.

2 Ladle jam into half-pint freezer containers, leaving a ½-inch headspace. Seal and label. Let stand at room temperature for 24 hours before serving. Store for up to 3 weeks in the refrigerator or for up to 1 year in the freezer. **Makes about 5 half-pints.**

PER TABLESPOON: 46 cal., 0 g fat, 0 mg chol., 1 mg sodium, 12 g carbo., 0 g fiber, 0 g pro.

TEST KITCHEN tip

Peak kiwifruit season spans from November through May. The green-flesh kiwi is the most common, but there is also the gold kiwi—which is less hairy than green kiwi. It has bright gold flesh and a flavor reminiscent of honey.

Pineapple-Coconut Sauce

Use this versatile sauce as a dessert topping or as a dipping sauce for crispy coconut shrimp.

PREP: 35 minutes   **STAND:** 10 minutes + 24 hours

4   cups sugar
2   cups finely chopped fresh
    pineapple
1   1.75-ounce package regular
    powdered fruit pectin
¾   cup water
¾   cup finely chopped toasted
    coconut

1 In a large bowl stir together sugar and pineapple. Let stand at room temperature for 10 minutes, stirring occasionally. In a small saucepan stir pectin into the water. Bring to boiling over high heat. Boil hard for 1 minute, stirring constantly. Add pectin mixture to pineapple mixture, stirring about 3 minutes or until sugar dissolves and mixture is not grainy. Stir in coconut.

2 Ladle sauce into half-pint freezer containers, leaving a ½-inch headspace. Seal and label. Let stand at room temperature for 24 hours before serving. Store for up to 3 weeks in the refrigerator or for up to 1 year in the freezer. **Makes about 5 half-pints.**

PER 2 TABLESPOONS: 96 cal., 1 g fat (1 g sat. fat), 0 mg chol., 8 mg sodium, 23 g carbo., 0 g fiber, 0 g pro.

To toast coconut, spread it in a single layer in a shallow rimmed baking pan. Toast in a 350°F oven for 5 to 10 minutes, shaking and stirring it once. Watch it carefully—its high fat and sugar content means it burns easily.

Brown Sugar-Vanilla Banana Butter

This rich, sweet, and silky fruit butter—punctuated with crunchy toasted pecans—makes an exquisite topping for waffles, pancakes, and popovers.

PREP: 30 minutes   **COOK:** 15 minutes   **PROCESS:** 5 minutes

- 4 cups packed brown sugar
- 2 cups granulated sugar
- 4 cups mashed bananas (about 12 ripe bananas)
- ½ cup lemon juice
- 1 1.75-ounce box regular powdered fruit pectin
- ½ teaspoon butter
- 1 vanilla bean, split lengthwise
- 1 cup toasted chopped pecans (optional)

1 In a large bowl combine brown sugar and granulated sugar; set aside. In a 6- to 8-quart heavy pot combine mashed bananas, lemon juice, pectin, and butter. Scrape the seeds from the vanilla bean; add the seeds and the pod to the pot. Bring mixture to a full rolling boil over high heat, stirring constantly.

2 Stir in sugar all at once. Boil hard for 1 minute, stirring constantly. Remove and discard vanilla bean pod. If desired, stir in pecans.

3 Ladle hot mixture into hot, sterilized half-pint canning jars, leaving a ¼-inch headspace. Wipe jar rims; adjust lids.

4 Process filled jars in a boiling-water canner for 5 minutes (start timing when water returns to boiling). Remove jars from canner; cool on wire racks. **Makes about 9 half-pints.**

PER TABLESPOON: 44 cal., 0 g fat, 0 mg chol., 2 mg sodium, 11 g carbo., 0 g fiber, 0 g pro.

TEST KITCHEN tip

Bananas mash much easier when they're a little overripe. Use bananas that are speckled all over and slightly soft to the touch for this recipe. The simplest way to mash the bananas is with an old-fashioned potato masher.

CHAPTER 8

First Blush

When touched by the summer sun, apricots, nectarines, peaches, and plums become flush with tantalizing aromas and juicy goodness. Even better, the fruits preserve magnificently.

CARDAMOM-PEACH JAM

SWEET BASIL-PEACH JAM

CHIPOTLE-PEACH JAM

BOURBON-PEACH JAM

Peach Jam

Make quick work of chopping the peaches: Place small batches of peeled and cut-up peaches in a food processor. Cover and pulse until peaches are finely chopped.

PREP: 30 minutes   **PROCESS:** 5 minutes

7	cups sugar
4	cups finely chopped, peeled ripe peaches (about 3 pounds fresh) (see tip, page 139)
¼	cup lemon juice
½	of a 6-ounce package (1 foil pouch) liquid fruit pectin

1 In a 6- to 8-quart heavy pot combine sugar, peaches, and lemon juice. Bring to boiling, stirring constantly until sugar dissolves. Quickly stir in pectin. Bring to a full rolling boil, stirring constantly. Boil hard for 1 minute, stirring constantly. Remove from heat. Quickly skim off foam with a metal spoon.

2 Ladle hot jam into hot, sterilized half-pint canning jars, leaving a ¼-inch headspace. Wipe jar rims; adjust lids.

3 Process filled jars in a boiling-water canner for 5 minutes (start timing when water returns to boiling). Remove jars from canner; cool on wire racks. To distribute fruit, cool for about 20 minutes, then gently turn and tilt jars without inverting them; repeat as needed. **Makes about 7 half-pints.**

PER TABLESPOON: 54 cal., 0 g fat, 0 mg chol., 0 mg sodium, 14 g carbo., 0 g fiber, 0 g pro.

Cardamom-Peach Jam: Prepare as directed, except stir in ¾ teaspoon freshly ground cardamom after skimming off foam.

Sweet Basil-Peach Jam: Prepare as directed, except stir in 1 cup snipped fresh basil after skimming off foam.

Bourbon-Peach Jam: Prepare as directed, except stir in ½ cup bourbon with the sugar, peaches, and lemon juice.

Chipotle-Peach Jam: Prepare as directed, except stir in 2 finely chopped chipotle chile peppers in adobo sauce (see tip, page 57) with the sugar, peaches, and lemon juice.

Peach Bellini Jam

To make a peach Bellini float, combine this magnificent jam with soda water and a couple scoops of vanilla ice cream.

PREP: 45 minutes **PROCESS:** 5 minutes

7½ cups sugar
3 cups finely chopped, peeled ripe peaches (see tip, page 139)
1 cup Prosecco or other sparkling white wine
2 tablespoons lemon juice
½ of a 6-ounce package (1 foil pouch) liquid fruit pectin

1 In a 6- to 8-quart stainless-steel, enamel, or nonstick heavy pot combine sugar, peaches, Prosecco, and lemon juice. Bring to a full rolling boil, stirring constantly until sugar dissolves. Quickly stir in liquid pectin. Return to a full rolling boil, stirring constantly. Boil hard for 1 minute, stirring constantly. Remove from heat. Quickly skim off foam with a metal spoon, avoiding peaches.

2 Ladle hot jam into hot, sterilized half-pint canning jars, leaving a ¼-inch headspace. Wipe jar rims; adjust lids.

3 Process filled jars in a boiling-water canner for 5 minutes (start timing when water returns to boiling). Remove jars from canner; cool on wire racks. To distribute fruit, cool for about 20 minutes, then gently turn and tilt jars without inverting them; repeat as needed. **Makes 8 half-pints.**

PER TABLESPOON: 49 cal., 0 g fat, 0 mg chol., 0 mg sodium, 12 g carbo., 0 g fiber, 0 g pro.

Nectarine and Vanilla Bean Jam

Use the tip of a small, sharp paring knife to split the vanilla beans.

PREP: 1 hour   **PROCESS:** 5 minutes

4	cups chopped peeled ripe nectarines (see tip, page 139)
¼	cup lemon juice
2	vanilla beans, split lengthwise
7	cups sugar
½	of a 6-ounce package (1 foil pouch) liquid fruit pectin

1 In a 6- to 8-quart heavy pot combine nectarines and lemon juice. Using a potato masher, crush the nectarines to create a pulp. Scrape the seeds from the vanilla beans into the pot. Stir in the vanilla bean pods and the sugar. Bring mixture to boiling over medium heat, stirring constantly until sugar dissolves.

2 Increase heat to medium-high; bring mixture to a full rolling boil, stirring constantly. Quickly stir in pectin. Return to a full rolling boil, stirring constantly. Boil hard for 1 minute. Remove from heat. Quickly skim off foam with a metal spoon. Remove and discard vanilla bean pods.

3 Ladle hot jam into hot, sterilized half-pint canning jars, leaving a ¼-inch headspace. Wipe jar rims; adjust lids.

4 Process filled jars in a boiling-water canner for 5 minutes (start timing when water returns to boiling). Remove jars from canner; cool on wire racks. To distribute fruit, cool for about 20 minutes, then gently turn and tilt jars without inverting; repeat as needed. **Makes 6 half-pints.**

PER TABLESPOON: 65 cal., 0 g fat, 0 mg chol., 0 mg sodium, 17 g carbo., 0 g fiber, 0 g pro.

Can It!

Jalapeño-Peach Jelly

Upgrade the classic peanut butter and jelly sandwich by spreading it with cashew butter and plenty of this spiced-up peach jelly.

PREP: 40 minutes   **COOK:** 20 minutes   **PROCESS:** 5 minutes   **STAND:** 2 days

2 pounds peaches, peeled, pitted, and chopped (see tip, page 139)
1 cup cider vinegar
3 to 4 fresh jalapeño chile peppers, seeded (if desired) and coarsely chopped (see tip, page 57)
5 cups sugar
½ of a 6-ounce package (1 foil pouch) liquid fruit pectin

1 In a large stainless-steel, enamel, or nonstick saucepan use a potato masher to crush peaches. Add vinegar and chile peppers. Bring to boiling over high heat; reduce heat. Simmer, covered, for about 20 minutes or until peaches and peppers are very soft. Using a jelly bag or a colander lined with several layers of 100%-cotton cheesecloth, strain the mixture. You should have about 2 cups strained liquid. Discard solids.

2 In the same large saucepan combine the 2 cups strained liquid and the sugar. Bring to a full rolling boil over high heat, stirring constantly. Quickly stir in pectin. Return to a full rolling boil. Boil hard for 1 minute, stirring constantly. Remove from heat. Skim off foam with a metal spoon.

3 Ladle hot jelly into hot, sterilized half-pint canning jars, leaving a ¼-inch headspace. Wipe jar rims; adjust lids.

4 Process filled jars in a boiling-water canner for 5 minutes (start timing when water returns to boiling). Remove jars from canner; cool on wire racks. Before serving, let jelly stand at room temperature for 2 to 3 days or until jelly is set. **Makes 5 half-pints.**

PER TABLESPOON: 54 cal., 0 g fat, 0 mg chol., 0 mg sodium, 14 g carbo., 0 g fiber, 0 g pro.

Can It!

Peach Melba Jelly

This peach and raspberry jelly creates the perfect filling for small donuts such as sufganiyot (left), which are traditional treats served during Hanukkah.

PREP: 20 minutes   **PROCESS:** 5 minutes

2½   **cups peach nectar**
1   **cup raspberry puree (see tip, below)**
¼   **cup lemon juice**
7½   **cups sugar**
1   **6-ounce package (2 foil pouches) liquid fruit pectin**

1 In an 8-quart stainless-steel, enamel, or nonstick heavy pot combine peach nectar, raspberry puree, and lemon juice. Stir in sugar. Bring to a full rolling boil, stirring constantly. Quickly stir in pectin. Return to a full rolling boil, stirring constantly. Boil hard for 1 minute, stirring constantly. Remove from heat. Quickly skim off foam with a metal spoon.

2 Ladle hot jelly into hot, sterilized half-pint canning jars, leaving a ¼-inch headspace. Wipe jar rims; adjust lids.

3 Process filled jars in a boiling-water canner for 5 minutes (start timing when water returns to boiling). Remove jars from canner; cool on wire racks. **Makes 10 half-pints.**

PER TABLESPOON: 39 cal., 0 g fat, 0 mg chol., 1 mg sodium, 10 g carbo., 0 g fiber, 0 g pro.

TEST KITCHEN *tip*

For raspberry puree, place 3 cups fresh raspberries in a blender. Cover and blend until berries are smooth. Press blended berries through a fine-mesh sieve; discard seeds. Measure 1 cup sieved puree.

Can It!

Peach-Honey Butter

This honey-sweetened spread tastes delicious with just about every kind of cookie and cracker, but it is especially good on almond biscotti—either homemade or purchased.

PREP: 35 minutes   **COOK:** 20 minutes   **PROCESS:** 5 minutes

18	medium ripe peaches, peeled, pitted, and cut up (see tip, below)
¼	cup water
2¼	cups sugar
¾	cup honey

1 In an 8- to 10-quart heavy pot combine peaches and the water. Bring to boiling; reduce heat. Simmer, covered, for 10 to 15 minutes or until peaches are tender. Remove from heat. Cool slightly.

2 Use a blender to puree peach mixture, in batches, until smooth. Return peach puree to same pot. Add sugar and honey. Bring to boiling, stirring until sugar dissolves; reduce heat. Simmer, uncovered, for about 10 minutes or until mixture is thick and mounds on a spoon, stirring often.

3 Ladle hot butter into hot, sterilized half-pint canning jars, leaving a ¼-inch headspace. Wipe jar rims; adjust lids.

4 Process filled jars in a boiling-water canner for 5 minutes (start timing when water returns to boiling). Remove jars from canner; cool on wire racks. **Makes 4 half-pints.**

PER TABLESPOON: 56 cal., 0 g fat, 0 mg chol., 0 mg sodium, 14 g carbo., 1 g fiber, 0 g pro.

TEST KITCHEN tip

To peel peaches, nectarines, and apricots, bring a large pot of water to boiling. Place fruit in boiling water for 30 to 60 seconds or until skins start to split. Remove fruit from boiling water with a slotted spoon and plunge into a bowl of ice water. Remove fruit from water after a few minutes and use a knife to easily pull off the skins.

SPICED
Peaches

Spiced Peaches

Select ripe, ready-to-eat peaches. Look for freestone peaches, which are easiest to prepare because the flesh does not cling to the pit.

PREP: 40 minutes   **COOL:** 30 minutes   **PROCESS:** 25 minutes

5¼	**cups water**
2¼	**cups sugar**
12	**whole cloves**
2	**3- to 4-inch cinnamon sticks**
8	**to 10 pounds ripe peaches**
	Ascorbic-acid color keeper
	(see page 17)

1 For syrup, in a 4- to 6-quart heavy pot combine the water, sugar, cloves, and cinnamon sticks. Bring to boiling, stirring until sugar dissolves; reduce heat. Simmer, uncovered, for 5 minutes, stirring occasionally. Cool for 30 minutes. Using a slotted spoon, remove and discard cinnamon sticks. If desired, remove cloves from syrup. Set syrup aside.

2 Bring a large saucepan of water to boiling. Fill a large bowl with ice water. Carefully lower 2 or 3 peaches into the boiling water for 30 to 60 seconds. Using a slotted spoon, transfer peaches from boiling water to the ice water. When peaches are cool enough to handle, remove and discard skins. Repeat with remaining peaches.

3 Cut peaches in half. Remove and discard pits. Slice peaches. To prevent discoloration, place peach slices immediately into ascorbic-acid color keeper solution. Pack peach slices into hot, sterilized quart canning jars, leaving a ½-inch headspace.

4 Return syrup to boiling. Ladle hot syrup into jars, covering peaches and maintaining the ½-inch headspace. Remove air bubbles. Wipe jar rims; adjust lids.

5 Process filled jars in a boiling-water canner for 25 minutes (start timing when water returns to boiling). Remove jars from canner; cool on wire racks. **Makes 5 quarts.**

PER ¾ CUP: 127 cal., 0 g fat, 0 mg chol., 1 mg sodium, 32 g carbo., 2 g fiber, 1 g pro.

Butter-Spiced Nectarines

These buttery stone fruits deliciously adorn challah or brioche. Label the jars with directions to warm the nectarine mixture before serving—especially if you are giving them as gifts.

PREP: 45 minutes   **PROCESS:** 15 minutes

½   **cup butter**
½   **cup sugar**
4   **pounds ripe nectarines, peeled if desired (see tip, page 139), pitted, and each cut into 8 wedges**
½   **cup water**
2   **tablespoons lemon juice**
1   **teaspoon ground cinnamon**
¼   **teaspoon ground nutmeg**
¼   **teaspoon ground cloves**

1 In a 4- to 5-quart heavy pot combine butter and sugar; cook over medium heat for 5 to 8 minutes or until mixture begins to brown, stirring constantly. Add nectarine wedges to butter mixture, stirring to coat. Cook and stir about 4 minutes or just until nectarines begin to soften, gently stirring occasionally. Stir in the water, lemon juice, cinnamon, nutmeg, and cloves. Bring to boiling; boil for 1 minute. Remove from heat.

2 Ladle hot mixture into hot, sterilized half-pint canning jars, evenly distributing nectarines and liquid and leaving a ¼-inch headspace. Wipe jar rims; adjust lids.

3 Process filled jars in a boiling-water canner for 15 minutes (start timing when water returns to boiling). Remove jars from canner; cool on wire racks. **Makes about 9 half-pints.**

PER ¼ CUP: 54 cal., 3 g fat (2 g sat. fat), 7 mg chol., 18 mg sodium, 8 g carbo., 1 g fiber, 1 g pro.

Balsamic Pickled Apricots

Enjoy these radiantly-hued treats with roast pork at dinnertime or serve them alongside a breakfast strata for brunch.

PREP: 35 minutes **STAND:** 30 minutes **PROCESS:** 10 minutes

1 cup white balsamic vinegar
½ cup sweet vermouth
½ cup honey
½ cup water
2 3-inch sticks cinnamon, broken
6 whole cloves
2 pounds ripe apricots

1 For syrup, in a medium stainless-steel, enamel, or nonstick heavy saucepan combine vinegar, vermouth, honey, the water, cinnamon, and cloves. Bring to boiling; reduce heat. Simmer, uncovered, for 5 minutes. Remove from heat; let stand for 30 minutes. Remove and discard cinnamon sticks and cloves.

2 Fill a large saucepan with water; bring to boiling. Fill a large bowl with ice water. Carefully lower apricots into the boiling water for 30 to 60 seconds. Using a slotted spoon, transfer apricots from boiling water to ice water. When apricots are cool enough to handle, remove and discard skins.

3 Cut each apricot in half and remove pit. Halve each apricot half. Pack apricot quarters into hot, sterilized half-pint canning jars, leaving a ½-inch headspace.

4 Return syrup to boiling. Pour hot syrup over apricots to cover, maintaining the ½-inch headspace. Remove air bubbles. Wipe jar rims; adjust lids.

5 Process filled jars in a boiling-water canner for 10 minutes (start timing when water returns to boiling). Remove jars from canner; cool on wire racks. **Makes 5 half-pints.**

PER ¼ CUP: 67 cal., 0 g fat, 0 mg chol., 4 mg sodium, 15 g carbo., 1 g fiber, 1 g pro.

Balsamic Pickled Plums: Prepare as directed above, except substitute dark balsamic vinegar for the white balsamic vinegar and substitute plums for the apricots. Do not peel the plums.

Apricot-Date Chutney

For little party appetizers, make cocktail rye sandwiches with a bit of cream cheese and this spicy condiment. Or complement baked ham or turkey breast with the chutney.

PREP: 40 minutes   **COOK:** 15 minutes   **PROCESS:** 10 minutes

1	tablespoon vegetable oil
1	cup chopped onion (1 large)
2	teaspoons grated fresh ginger
4	cloves garlic, minced
⅔	cup sugar
½	cup red wine vinegar
¼	cup lemon juice
½	teaspoon dry mustard
½	teaspoon ground allspice
	Dash ground cloves
3	cups chopped, peeled ripe apricots (8 to 12 medium) (see tip, page 139)
¾	cup snipped, pitted dates

1 In a medium stainless-steel, enamel, or nonstick heavy saucepan heat oil over medium heat. Add onion, ginger, and garlic. Cook until onion is tender, stirring occasionally. Stir in sugar, vinegar, lemon juice, mustard, allspice, and cloves. Bring to boiling, stirring to dissolve sugar; reduce heat. Simmer, uncovered, for 5 minutes.

2 Stir apricots and dates into the onion mixture. Return to boiling; reduce heat. Simmer, uncovered, for about 10 minutes or until mixture is thickened, stirring occasionally. Remove from heat.

3 Ladle hot chutney into hot, sterilized half-pint canning jars, leaving a ½-inch headspace. Wipe jar rims; adjust lids.

4 Process filled jars in a boiling-water canner for 10 minutes (start timing when water returns to boiling). Remove jars from canner; cool on wire racks. **Makes 4 half-pints.**

PER 2 TABLESPOONS: 39 cal., 0 g fat, 0 mg chol., 1 mg sodium, 9 g carbo., 1 g fiber, 0 g pro.

TEST KITCHEN *tip*

If you live far from stone-fruit territory, rely on your supermarket produce manager to let you know when crates of the luscious fruits arrive from California, Georgia, and Colorado's West Slope. In general, apricots arrive from May to August.

Pickled Plums

These beauties are plumb dandy served with roast pork, barbecued shrimp, or Asian-inspired grilled chicken.

PREP: 35 minutes   **PROCESS:** 5 minutes

3½	pounds medium red, purple, and/or green plums (about 14)
2	medium red onions
2	cups water
2	cups red wine vinegar
2½	cups sugar
2	3- to 4-inch cinnamon sticks
8	whole allspice
4	whole cloves
2	star anise
½	teaspoon salt

1 Wash plums. Cut the plums in half; pit. Remove root and stem ends from onions. Cut the onions in half lengthwise; cut into ½-inch-thick slices. Pack the plum halves and onion slices into hot, sterilized pint canning jars.

2 In a large stainless-steel, enamel, or nonstick heavy saucepan combine the water and vinegar. Bring to boiling. Add sugar, cinnamon, allspice, cloves, star anise, and salt. Return to boiling, stirring until sugar dissolves. Remove from heat.

3 Pour hot liquid over plums and onions in jars, leaving a ¼-inch headspace. Wipe jar rims; adjust lids.

4 Process filled jars in a boiling-water canner for 5 minutes (start timing when water returns to boiling). Remove jars from canner; cool on wire racks. **Makes 5 pints.**

PER ½ CUP: 239 cal., 0 g total fat, 0 mg chol., 102 mg sodium, 59 g carbo., 2 g fiber, 1 g pro.

TEST KITCHEN *tip*

Here's how to pick perfect plums: Look for fruit that yields to gentle pressure and that is free of blemishes. Good-quality plums will have rich color and will retain a slight whitish bloom, a sign that they have not been overhandled.

Peppered Plum Jam

For a quick and easy appetizer, melt a bit of this sweet-spicy jam to use as a glaze on baked chicken wings.

PREP: 35 minutes **PROCESS:** 5 minutes

4	pounds plums
½	cup water
8	cups sugar
1	1.75-ounce package regular powdered fruit pectin
2	teaspoons freshly cracked black pepper

1 Pit and finely chop plums (do not peel). In a 5- to 6-quart heavy pot combine plums and the water. Bring to boiling; reduce heat. Simmer, covered, for 5 minutes. Remove pot from heat. Measure 6 cups cooked plums; return to pot.

2 Add sugar to plum mixture. Bring to a full rolling boil, stirring constantly. Quickly stir in pectin. Return to a full rolling boil, stirring constantly. Boil hard for 1 minute, stirring constantly. Remove from heat. Stir in pepper.

3 Ladle hot jam into hot, sterilized half-pint canning jars, leaving a ¼-inch headspace. Wipe jar rims; adjust lids.

4 Process filled jars in a boiling-water canner for 5 minutes (start timing when water returns to boiling). Remove jars from canner; cool on wire racks. **Makes 10 half-pints.**

PER TABLESPOON: 45 cal., 0 gl fat, 0 mg chol., 0 mg sodium, 12 g carbo., 0 g fiber, 0 g pro.

TEST KITCHEN
tip

You can either buy cracked pepper in a jar or simply turn the knob on your pepper grinder to the loosest setting to make your own freshly cracked black pepper.

CHAPTER 9

Row Crops

Crisp green beans, sweet-kernel corn, and peppers lay the groundwork for bushels of culinary creativity.
Learn how to capture their summery essence in a jar.

Pickled Dilled Green Beans

These make a delicious accompaniment to hearty grilled steak or roast beef. For spicier green bean pickles, add a whole chile pepper to each jar.

PREP: 45 minutes   **COOK:** 5 minutes   **PROCESS:** 5 minutes

3	pounds fresh green beans
5	fresh Thai or red serrano chile peppers (optional) (see tip, page 57)
3	cups water
3	cups white wine vinegar
3	tablespoons snipped fresh dill or 1 tablespoon dried dill
1	tablespoon pickling salt
1	tablespoon sugar
6	cloves garlic, minced
½	teaspoon crushed red pepper or 1 Thai chile pepper
5	small heads fresh dill (optional)

1 Wash beans; drain. If desired, remove ends and strings. Leave beans whole. In an uncovered 8-quart pot cook beans and the 5 fresh chile peppers (if using) in enough boiling water to cover for 5 minutes; drain.

2 Pack hot beans lengthwise into hot, sterilized pint canning jars, cutting beans to fit if necessary and leaving a ½-inch headspace. Add 1 of the boiled chile peppers (if using) to each jar. Set aside.

3 In a large stainless-steel, enamel, or nonstick heavy saucepan combine water, vinegar, snipped or dried dill, pickling salt, sugar, garlic, and crushed red pepper. Bring to boiling, stirring until sugar dissolves.

4 Pour hot liquid over beans in jars, leaving a ½-inch headspace. If desired, add a head of fresh dill to each jar. Wipe jar rims; adjust lids.

5 Process filled jars in a boiling-water canner for 5 minutes (start timing when water returns to boiling). Remove jars from canner; cool on wire racks. **Makes 5 pints.**

PER ½ CUP: 42 cal., 0 g fat, 0 mg chol., 357 mg sodium, 7 g carbo., 3 g fiber, 2 g pro.

TEST KITCHEN *tip*

Use your choice of snap, wax, or Italian beans for these savory pickles. For the best flavor, let the jars stand in a cool, dark place for two weeks before serving or sharing the pickled beans.

Lemon-and-Bay Leaf Bean Pickles

Although they're good just for munching, these citrusy pickled green beans also provide a superb garnish for a spicy Bloody Mary.

PREP: 45 minutes   **PROCESS:** 10 minutes

2¾	cups water
2	cups white wine vinegar
½	cup sugar
⅓	cup lemon juice
1	tablespoon pickling salt
2¼	pounds fresh green and/or yellow beans, trimmed (about 11 cups)
8	bay leaves
4	teaspoons whole black peppercorns
8	strips lemon peel

1. In a 6- to 8-quart stainless-steel, enamel, or nonstick heavy pot combine the water, vinegar, sugar, lemon juice, and salt. Bring to boiling over medium-high heat, stirring constantly until sugar and salt dissolve. Add beans; return to boiling. Boil for 1 minute. Drain beans, reserving the liquid. Return reserved liquid to the pot. Return to a simmer; cover.

2. Pack hot beans lengthwise into hot, sterilized pint jars, adding 2 of the bay leaves, 1 teaspoon of the peppercorns, and 2 strips of the lemon peel to each jar.

3. Pour boiling liquid over beans in jars, leaving a ½-inch headspace. Remove any air bubbles from jars.

4. Process filled jars in a boiling-water canner for 10 minutes (start timing when water returns to boiling). Remove jars from canner; cool on wire racks. **Makes 4 pints.**

PER ¼ CUP: 27 cal., 0 g fat, 0 mg chol., 184 mg sodium, 6 g carbo., 1 g fiber, 1 g pro.

Farmer's Market Corn Salsa

Delicious as a dip for tortilla chips or as a topping for nachos, this creative corn concoction also tastes amazing with grilled chicken and a salad.

PREP: 35 minutes   **COOK:** 10 minutes   **PROCESS:** 15 minutes

4   large fresh ears corn
1   cup coarsely chopped onion (1 large)
1   cup coarsely chopped green or red sweet pepper (1 large)
1   cup chopped, peeled tomato
1   fresh jalapeño chile pepper, seeded and finely chopped (see tip, page 57)
½   cup lime juice
½   teaspoon salt
½   teaspoon ground cumin
½   teaspoon freshly ground black pepper

1 Remove husks from ears of corn. Scrub corn with a stiff vegetable brush to remove silks; rinse. Cut kernels from cobs (do not scrape cobs). Measure 2 cups of corn kernels.

2 In a large saucepan combine the 2 cups corn kernels, onion, sweet pepper, tomato, jalapeño pepper, lime juice, salt, cumin, and black pepper. Bring to boiling; reduce heat. Simmer, covered, for 10 minutes.

3 Ladle hot salsa into hot, sterilized half-pint canning jars, leaving a ½-inch headspace. Wipe jar rims; adjust lids.

4 Process filled jars in a boiling-water canner for 15 minutes (start timing when water returns to boiling). Remove jars from canner; cool on wire racks. **Makes about 4 half-pints.**

PER ¼ CUP: 48 cal., 1 g fat (0 g sat. fat), 0 mg chol., 0 mg sodium, 11 g carbo., 2 g fiber, 2 g pro.

TEST KITCHEN
tip

Look for ears of corn with tight-fitting bright green husks and golden brown silks. The rows of kernels should be tightly spaced and extend to the tips. Corn contains sugar that quickly begins turning to starch as soon as an ear is picked, so use corn as soon as possible after harvesting.

Pickled Green Chiles

Spice up shredded pork or beef for tacos with these lip-puckering pickled chiles—or make them part of a condiment tray of chili toppings.

PREP: 40 minutes **COOK:** 5 minutes **PROCESS:** 10 minutes **STAND:** 1 week at room temperature

1½   pounds fresh jalapeño and/or
     serrano peppers (see tip,
     page 57)
1½   pounds fresh poblano peppers
     (see tip, page 57)
3   cups water
3   cups white vinegar
1   cup white wine vinegar
2   tablespoons sugar
1   teaspoon pickling salt
6   cloves garlic

1 Thinly slice peppers into rings, discarding stem ends, excess seeds, and membranes.

2 In a 4- to 5-quart stainless-steel, enamel, or nonstick heavy pot combine the water, white vinegar, white wine vinegar, sugar, and pickling salt. Bring mixture to boiling, stirring until sugar and salt dissolve.

3 Pack sliced peppers into hot, sterilized pint jars, leaving a ½-inch headspace. Place 1 clove garlic in each jar. Pour hot liquid over peppers, maintaining the ½-inch headspace. Discard any remaining vinegar mixture. Wipe jar rims; adjust lids.

4 Process jars in a boiling-water canner for 10 minutes (start timing when water returns to boiling). Remove jars from canner; cool on wire racks. Allow to stand at room temperature for 1 week before serving. **Makes 6 pints.**

PER ¼ CUP: 20 cal., 0 g fat, 0 mg chol., 43 mg sodium, 3 g carbo., 0 g fiber, 0 g pro.

TEST KITCHEN
tip

For perfectly even slices, use a mandoline to slice the chiles. It doesn't have to be a top-of-the-line stainless-steel model—which can cost more than $200. Perfectly practical and sturdy models made of hard plastic are available for under $30.

Spicy-Sweet Pickled Three-Bean Salad

This picnic-perfect salad is a bit like the version you see at nearly every supermarket deli—only so much better. Make it when wax beans are in season—midsummer to early fall.

PREP: 1 hour   **COOK:** 1 hour to 1 hour 30 minutes   **PROCESS:** 15 minutes   **STAND:** 1 week at room temperature

1¼   cups dried dark red kidney beans
1½   pounds green beans, trimmed and cut into 1½-inch pieces
1½   pounds wax beans, trimmed and cut into 1½-inch pieces
2   large onions, chopped
2   large red sweet peppers, chopped
2   jalapeno chile peppers, seeded and finely chopped (see tip, page 57)
6   cups sugar
4   cups white vinegar
3   cups water
1   cup cider vinegar
1   cup red wine vinegar
2   tablespoons pickling salt

1   Rinse kidney beans. In a large saucepan combine kidney beans and enough water to cover. Bring to boiling; reduce heat. Simmer, uncovered, for 2 minutes. Remove from heat. Cover; let stand for 1 hour. (Or soak dried beans in water overnight in a covered pan.) Drain kidney beans and rinse. In the same saucepan combine kidney beans and enough water to cover. Bring to boiling; reduce heat. Cover and simmer 1 to 1½ hours or until beans are tender; drain. Set aside to cool.

2   Fill a large pot about two-thirds full with water. Bring to boiling. Add green beans; blanch for 3 minutes. Transfer green beans to a large bowl of ice water. Repeat blanching process with wax beans. Drain green beans and wax beans from ice water. In a large bowl combine the green beans, wax beans, kidney beans, onions, sweet red peppers, and jalapeño peppers.

3   Meanwhile, in a large stainless-steel, enamel, or nonstick saucepan combine sugar, white vinegar, water, cider vinegar, red wine vinegar, and pickling salt. Bring to boiling, stirring until sugar and salt are dissolved.

4   Pack bean mixture into hot, sterilized pint jars, leaving a ½-inch headspace. Ladle hot vinegar mixture into jars, maintaining the ½ inch headspace. Discard any remaining vinegar mixture. Wipe jar rims; adjust lids.

5   Process filled jars in a boiling-water canner for 15 minutes (start timing when water returns to boiling). Remove jars from canner; cool on wire racks. Allow to stand at room temperature for 1 week before serving. **Makes 8 pints.**

PER ½ CUP: 240 cal., 0 g fat, 0 mg chol., 375 mg sodium, 53 g carbo., 4 g fiber, 5 g pro.

Mustardy Pickled Banana Pepper Rings

Swirling with mustard seeds, the jars of these sunny-hued pepper rings are beautiful just sitting on the shelf. But you do want to open them and enjoy—the peppers make a tasty addition to a juicy grilled steak.

PREP: 30 minutes   **COOK:** 5 minutes   **PROCESS:** 10 minutes   **STAND:** 1 week at room temperature

2 pounds sweet and/or hot banana peppers (see tip, page 57)
5 cups white vinegar
2 cups water
½ cup sugar
1 tablespoon dry mustard
4 cloves garlic, smashed
½ teaspoon ground turmeric
4 tablespoons yellow mustard seeds
4 tablespoons brown mustard seeds

1 Slice peppers into rings, discarding stem ends and excess seeds.

2 In a large stainless-steel, enamel, or nonstick saucepan combine vinegar, the water, sugar, dry mustard, garlic, and turmeric. Bring to boiling stirring to dissolve sugar; reduce heat and simmer for 5 minutes. Discard garlic.

3 Pack peppers into hot, sterilized pint jars, leaving a ½-inch headspace. Add 1 tablespoon each yellow and brown mustard seeds to each jar. Ladle hot vinegar mixture over peppers in jars, maintaining the ½-inch headspace. Discard any remaining vinegar mixture. Wipe jar rims; adjust lids.

4 Process jars in a boiling-water canner for 10 minutes (start timing when water returns to boiling). Remove jars from canner; cool on wire racks. Allow to stand at room temperature for 1 week before serving. **Makes 4 pints.**

PER ¼ CUP: 47 cal., 1 g fat (0 g sat. fat), 0 mg chol., 5 mg sodium, 6 g carbo., 1 g fiber, 1 g pro.

Canning can be done solo, but some of the most satisfying canning projects are done with friends and family. Get together a group and speed through the job while sharing a few hours of fun.

Can It!

Sweet-and-Sour Pickled Bell Peppers

This colorful pepper mix is delicious on deli-meat sandwiches—especially thinly sliced roast beef.

PREP: 30 minutes   **COOK:** 15 minutes   **PROCESS:** 10 minutes   **STAND:** 1 week

3   **pounds red, green, yellow, and/or orange sweet peppers**
2   **large onions, halved and thinly sliced**
4   **cups sugar**
4   **cups water**
3   **cups white vinegar**
2   **cups cider vinegar**
1   **tablespoon celery seeds**
1   **tablespoon whole black peppercorns**
1   **teaspoon mustard seeds**
4   **cloves garlic, smashed**
4   **bay leaves**
2   **teaspoons salt**

1 Remove stem end and seeds from each pepper. Slice lengthwise into strips. In a large bowl combine peppers and onions; set aside.

2 In a large stainless-steel, enamel, or nonstick saucepan combine sugar, water, white vinegar, cider vinegar, celery seeds, peppercorns, mustard seeds, garlic, bay leaves, and salt. Bring to boiling, stirring to dissolve the sugar and salt. Reduce heat to low and simmer, covered, for 15 to 20 minutes. Remove and discard garlic and bay leaves.

3 Pack pepper and onion mixture into hot, sterilized pint canning jars, leaving a ½-inch headspace. Pour hot vinegar mixture over pepper-onion mixture, leaving the ½-inch headspace. Discard any remaining hot vinegar mixture. Wipe jars rims and adjust lids.

4 Process filled jars in a boiling-water canner for 10 minutes (start timing when water returns to boiling). Remove jars from canner; cool on wire racks. Allow to stand at room temperature for 1 week. **Makes about 7 pints.**

PER ¼ CUP: 73 cal., 0 g fat, 0 mg chol., 86 mg sodium, 17 g carbo., 1 g fiber, 0 g pro.

TEST KITCHEN *tip*

You can make these pickled peppers with any combination of pepper colors—or all one color. The more colors you use, of course, the more eye-catching the final product.

CHAPTER 10

Apples & Pears

Orchards are autumn's jewelry boxes. Harvest a heap of crisp red, green, or golden apples or pears and discover how beautifully they bound from bushel to jar.

Applesauce

Make the simple and comforting basic recipe—or try one of the fancier versions pumped up with herbs, liqueur, or spices. Any of the varieties dress up crispy potato pancakes.

PREP: 1 hour   **COOK:** 25 minutes   **PROCESS:** 15 minutes for pints, 20 minutes for quarts

8	**pounds tart cooking apples (about 24 medium)**
2	**cups water**
10	**inches stick cinnamon (optional)**
¾	**to 1¼ cups sugar**

1 Core and quarter apples. In an 8- to 10-quart heavy pot combine apples, the water, and, if desired, stick cinnamon. Bring to boiling; reduce heat. Simmer, covered, for 25 to 35 minutes or until apples are very tender, stirring often.

2 Remove and discard cinnamon (if using). Press apples through a food mill or sieve. Return pulp to pot; discard solids. Stir in enough of the sugar to sweeten as desired. If necessary, stir in ½ to 1 cup water to make desired consistency. Bring to boiling, stirring constantly.

3 Ladle hot applesauce into hot, sterilized pint or quart canning jars, leaving a ½-inch headspace. Wipe jar rims; adjust lids.

4 Process filled jars in a boiling-water canner for 15 minutes for pints or 20 minutes for quarts (start timing when water returns to boiling). Remove jars from canner; cool on wire racks. **Makes 6 pints or 3 quarts.**

PER ½ CUP: 112 cal., 1 g fat (0 g sat. fat), 0 mg chol., 1 mg sodium, 29 g carbo., 4 g fiber, 0 g pro.

Browned Butter and Sage Applesauce: In a small saucepan heat 1 cup butter over low heat until melted. Continue heating until butter turns a light golden brown. Remove from heat. Prepare applesauce as directed, except omit the cinnamon and stir the browned butter and ½ cup snipped fresh sage in with the sugar.

Calvados-Cranberry Applesauce: Prepare as directed, except stir in 1 cup Calvados or other apple brandy and 1 cup dried cranberries or golden raisins with the sugar.

Ginger-Honey Applesauce: Prepare as directed, except substitute honey for the sugar. Stir in 1 cup finely chopped crystallized ginger before ladling into jars.

Apple Butter

A spoonful of this creamy spiced fruit butter turns a plain ham and cheese sandwich into something special.

PREP: 45 minutes   **COOK:** 2 hours   **PROCESS:** 5 minutes

4½	pounds tart cooking apples (about 14 medium)
4	cups apple cider or apple juice
2	cups sugar
2	tablespoons lemon juice (optional)
1½	teaspoons ground cinnamon
½	teaspoon ground allspice
¼	teaspoon ground cloves

1 Core and quarter unpeeled apples. In an 8- to 10-quart heavy pot combine apples and cider. Bring to boiling; reduce heat. Simmer, covered, for 30 to 35 minutes or until apples are very tender, stirring often.

2 Press apple mixture through a food mill or sieve. Return 9½ cups of the pulp to the pot. (If you have leftover apple mixture, chill it and serve it as applesauce.)

3 Stir in sugar, lemon juice (if using), cinnamon, allspice, and cloves. Bring to boiling; reduce heat. Cook, uncovered, over very low heat for 1½ to 1¾ hours or until mixture is very thick and mounds on a spoon, stirring often.

4 Ladle hot butter into hot, sterilized half-pint canning jars, leaving a ¼-inch headspace. Wipe jar rims; adjust lids.

5 Process filled jars in a boiling-water canner for 5 minutes (start timing when water returns to boiling). Remove jars from canner; cool on wire racks. **Makes 6 half-pints.**

PER TABLESPOON: 35 cal., 0 g fat, 0 mg chol., 0 mg sodium, 9 g carbo., 0 g fiber, 0 g pro.

FREEZER DIRECTIONS: Prepare as directed through Step 3. Place pot of apple butter in a sink filled with ice water; stir mixture to cool. Ladle apple butter into wide-mouth freezer containers, leaving a ½-inch headspace. Seal and label. Freeze for up to 10 months. Apple butter might darken with freezing.

Nutmeg-Apple Conserve

Top your morning oatmeal with this sweet conserve made with tart cooking apples. Good varieties to try include Granny Smith, McIntosh, and Jonathan.

PREP: 45 minutes   **COOK:** 10 minutes   **PROCESS:** 5 minutes

5	cups chopped, peeled tart cooking apples
1	cup water
⅓	cup lemon juice
1	1.75-ounce package regular powdered fruit pectin
4	cups sugar
1	cup golden raisins
½	teaspoon ground nutmeg

1 In a 6- to 8-quart heavy pot combine apples, the water, and lemon juice. Bring to boiling; reduce heat. Simmer, covered, for 10 minutes.

2 Stir in pectin. Bring mixture to a full rolling boil, stirring constantly. Stir in sugar and raisins. Return to a full rolling boil, stirring constantly. Boil hard for 1 minute, stirring constantly. Remove from heat. Stir in nutmeg. Quickly skim off foam with a metal spoon.

3 Ladle hot conserve into hot, sterilized half-pint canning jars, leaving a ¼-inch headspace. Wipe rims; adjust lids.

4 Process filled jars in a boiling-water canner for 5 minutes (start timing when water returns to boiling). Remove jars from canner; cool on wire racks. **Makes 6 half-pints.**

PER TABLESPOON: 49 cal., 0 g fat, 0 mg chol., 1 mg sodium, 13 g carbo., 0 g fiber, 0 g pro.

TEST KITCHEN *tip*

The peak seasons for apples and pears vary by region. Call local orchards to learn when they offer freshly harvested fruits. Supermarkets carry the best apples and pears in September and October.

Pear and Cranberry Conserve

Make a tasty and healthful vinaigrette by whisking together ¼ cup Pear and Cranberry Conserve, 2 tablespoons white balsamic vinegar, and 1 tablespoon olive oil. Serve over mixed greens.

PREP: 25 minutes   **COOK:** 20 minutes   **PROCESS:** 10 minutes

6	medium to large firm, ripe pears, such as Bartlett or Bosc (about 3 pounds total)
1	16-ounce package cranberries
4	cups sugar
1¼	cups water
2	tablespoons lemon juice
2	tablespoons finely shredded orange peel
⅛	teaspoon ground cinnamon
⅛	teaspoon ground allspice

1 Peel, core, and chop pears. In a 5- to 6-quart heavy pot combine pears, cranberries, sugar, the water, lemon juice, orange peel, cinnamon, and allspice. Bring to boiling over medium heat, stirring until sugar dissolves. Boil gently, stirring frequently, for 20 to 25 minutes or until mixture is thickened and sheets off a metal spoon (see tip, below).

2 Ladle hot pear mixture into hot, sterilized half-pint canning jars, leaving a ½-inch headspace. Wipe jar rims; adjust lids.

3 Process filled jars in a boiling-water canner for 10 minutes (start timing when water returns to boiling). Remove jars from canner; cool on wire racks. **Makes 7 half-pints.**

PER TABLESPOON: 37 cal., 0 g fat, 0 mg chol., 0 mg sodium, 10 g carbo., 1 g fiber, 0 g pro.

TEST KITCHEN
tip

To check if a mixture sheets, dip a metal spoon into the boiling mixture and hold it over the pan. When it is the right consistency, it will slide in sheets (rather than drips) from the spoon.

Rosemary-Pear Preserves

Pears are in season in late fall, so if you missed the summer canning season, you still have time to make home-preserved fruit for the holidays. Spread the herbed pear preserves over waffles for a special breakfast.

PREP: 55 minutes   **COOK:** 20 minutes
PROCESS: 10 minutes

4   **to 6 pounds firm, ripe Bartlett or Bosc pears (about 10 medium)**
3   **cups sugar**
1   **cup honey**
2   **teaspoons finely shredded lemon peel**
½   **cup lemon juice**
2   **teaspoons snipped fresh rosemary**

1 Core and peel pears. Finely chop enough pears to measure 8 cups. In a 4- to 5-quart heavy pot combine pears, sugar, honey, lemon peel, and lemon juice. Bring to boiling, stirring until sugar dissolves. Stir in rosemary. Simmer, uncovered, for 20 to 25 minutes or until mixture sheets off a metal spoon (see tip, page 177), stirring often. Remove from heat. Quickly skim off foam with a metal spoon.

2 Ladle hot preserves into hot, sterilized half-pint canning jars, leaving a ½-inch headspace. Wipe jar rims; adjust lids.

3 Process filled jars in a boiling-water canner for 10 minutes (start timing when water returns to boiling). Remove jars from canner; cool on wire racks. **Makes 7 half-pints.**

PER TABLESPOON: 44 cal., 0 g fat, 0 mg chol., 0 mg sodium, 12 g carbo., 1 g fiber, 0 g pro.

Golden Pear Chutney

For an effortless appetizer, serve the chutney alongside a wedge of blue cheese and toasted baguette slices.

PREP: 20 minutes   **COOK:** 15 minutes

COOL: 15 minutes   **CHILL:** 2 hours

1¼	cups pear nectar or apple juice
⅔	cup water
¼	cup cider vinegar
1	cup snipped dried pears
⅓	cup snipped dried apricots
½	cup very finely chopped onion
⅓	cup golden raisins
1	tablespoon sugar
1	tablespoon grated fresh ginger
¼	teaspoon crushed red pepper
1	tablespoon finely chopped crystallized ginger

1 In a heavy medium saucepan combine pear nectar, the water, vinegar, dried pears, dried apricots, onion, raisins, sugar, grated fresh ginger, and crushed red pepper. Bring to boiling; reduce heat. Simmer, uncovered, for 15 to 20 minutes or until fruit is soft, onion is tender, and most of the liquid is absorbed, stirring occasionally.

2 Remove from heat; cool for 15 minutes. Stir in crystallized ginger. Cover and chill in the refrigerator for at least 2 hours before serving.

3 Ladle chutney into a hot, sterilized half-pint jar, leaving a ½-inch headspace. Seal and label. (Place any remaining chutney in an airtight storage container.) Store in the refrigerator for up to 5 days. To freeze, transfer to a freezer-safe container. Seal and label. Freeze for up to 3 months. **Makes about 2 cups.**

PER TABLESPOON: 56 cal., 0 g fat, 0 mg chol., 3 mg sodium, 15 g carbo., 1 g fiber, 0 g pro.

CHAPTER 11

From the Herb Garden

Fresh herbs add a sensational flair of liveliness to all they touch. Use the summer's abundance of fragrant herbal greenery to create dazzling jellies, preserves, and compotes.

Herb Jelly

Make this unusual jelly with all of one kind of herb—such as basil, thyme, lemon verbena, or mint—or use a blend of different types. It's delicious spread on crackers with cream cheese.

PREP: 45 minutes **STAND:** 10 minutes **PROCESS:** 5 minutes

2 to 3 ounces assorted mixed fresh herb sprigs and/or edible flower petals (such as nasturtiums, pansies, violets, violas, roses, calendulas, marigolds, dianthuses, daylilies, and/or geraniums)

3 cups unsweetened apple juice

¼ cup lemon juice
Few drops yellow food coloring (optional)

1 1.75-ounce package regular powdered fruit pectin

4 cups sugar

1 Gently wash herb sprigs and/or flower petals in water. Drain; place herbs or petals on paper towels and gently blot. Chop herbs with stems attached. Place 1 to 1½ cups firmly packed chopped leaves and stems or flower petals in an 8- to 10-quart heavy pot. Add apple juice.

2 Bring mixture to boiling, stirring occasionally. Boil, uncovered, for 5 minutes. Remove from heat. Cover; let stand for 10 minutes.

3 Line a strainer or colander with a double layer of 100%-cotton cheesecloth; set colander over a large bowl. Strain herb and/or flower mixture through cheesecloth, pressing to extract all of the juice. Measure 3 cups juice mixture, adding additional apple juice if necessary. Discard stems, leaves, and petals.

4 In the same pot combine juice mixture, lemon juice, and, if desired, food coloring. Stir pectin into mixture in pot. Bring to a full rolling boil, stirring constantly. Add sugar. Return to a full rolling boil, stirring constantly. Boil hard for 1 minute, stirring constantly. Remove from heat. Skim off foam with a metal spoon.

5 Ladle hot jelly into hot, sterilized half-pint canning jars, leaving a ¼-inch headspace. Wipe jar rims; adjust lids.

6 Process filled jars in a boiling-water canner for 5 minutes (start timing when water returns to boiling). Remove jars from canner; cool on wire racks. **Makes 5 half-pints.**

PER TABLESPOON: 44 cal., 0 g fat, 0 mg chol., 2 mg sodium, 11 g carbo., 0 g fiber, 0 g pro.

Strawberry-Tarragon Preserves

These preserves add a radiant freshness to cookies, water crackers, and toast. If you don't have tarragon, fresh basil works equally well, adding a similar but milder licorice flavor to the preserves.

PREP: 50 minutes **STAND:** 2 hours **PROCESS:** 5 minutes

8	cups hulled, halved or quartered fresh strawberries (about 2½ pounds)
7	cups sugar
¼	cup lemon juice
½	teaspoon butter
1	6-ounce package (2 foil pouches) liquid fruit pectin
⅓	cup snipped fresh tarragon

1 In an 8-quart heavy pot gently stir together strawberries, 2 cups of the sugar, and the lemon juice. Cover and let stand for 2 hours.

2 Gradually stir in the remaining 5 cups sugar and the butter. Bring to a boil over medium heat, stirring constantly until sugar dissolves; reduce heat to low. Simmer gently, uncovered, for 2 minutes, stirring frequently.

3 Increase heat to medium-high and bring to a full rolling boil, stirring constantly. Quickly stir in pectin; return to boiling. Boil hard for 1 minute. Remove from heat. Quickly skim off foam with a metal spoon. Stir in tarragon.

4 Ladle hot preserves into hot, sterilized half-pint canning jars, leaving a ¼-inch headspace. Wipe jar rims; adjust lids.

5 Process filled jars in a boiling water canner for 5 minutes (start timing when water returns to boiling). Remove jars; cool on wire racks. To distribute fruit, cool for about 20 minutes, then gently turn and tilt jars without inverting them; repeat as needed. **Makes 5 half-pints.**

PER TABLESPOON: 41 cal., 0 g fat, 0 mg chol., 0 mg sodium, 10 g carbo., 0 g fiber, 0 g pro.

Spearmint-Orange Jelly

For a special occasion, serve this jelly alongside a roasted or grilled rack of lamb.

PREP: 25 minutes   **STAND:** 20 minutes   **PROCESS:** 5 minutes

1   cup loosely packed fresh
    spearmint leaves
2   cups orange juice
4   cups sugar
¼   cup cider vinegar or lemon juice
½   of a 6-ounce package (1 foil
    pouch) liquid fruit pectin

1 Place spearmint leaves in a medium bowl. In a large stainless-steel, enamel, or nonstick heavy saucepan bring orange juice to boiling; pour over mint leaves. Let stand at room temperature for 20 to 30 minutes. Using a fine-mesh sieve or paper coffee filter, strain juice into a small bowl, pressing mint to thoroughly extract liquid. Discard spearmint; return liquid to saucepan.

2 Add sugar and vinegar to liquid in saucepan. Bring to boiling, stirring until sugar dissolves. Quickly stir in pectin. Return to a full rolling boil. Boil hard for 1 minute, stirring constantly. Remove from heat. Quickly skim off foam with a metal spoon.

3 Ladle hot jelly into hot, sterilized half-pint canning jars, leaving a ¼-inch headspace. Wipe jar rims; adjust lids.

4 Process filled jars in a boiling-water canner for 5 minutes (start timing when water returns to boiling). Remove jars from canner; cool on wire racks. **Makes about 4 half-pint jars.**

PER TABLESPOON: 30 cal., 0 g fat, 0 mg chol., 0 mg sodium, 8 g carbo., 0 g fiber, 0 g pro.

TEST KITCHEN
tip

If you aren't able to use cut fresh herbs right away, trim the ends of the herb sprigs and place them in a tall glass jar. Fill the jar with enough cold water to cover 1 inch of the stems. Cover the jar with a clear plastic bag and store it in the refrigerator (or at room temperature for basil) for up to three days.

Blueberry and Lemon Verbena Compote

In the summer, layer this compote with scoops of lemon sorbet in a tall glass. For a warming fall appetizer, pour it over a baked Brie or Camembert.

PREP: 20 minutes   **COOK:** 25 minutes   **PROCESS:** 15 minutes

4 **cups blueberries**
3 **cups sugar**
¼ **cup water**
2 **teaspoons finely shredded lemon peel (set aside)**
3 **tablespoons lemon juice**
3 **tablespoons snipped fresh lemon verbena**

1 In a 6- to 8-quart heavy pot combine blueberries, sugar, the water, and lemon juice. Bring to boiling, stirring until sugar dissolves; reduce heat. Simmer, uncovered, for about 25 minutes or until mixture is thickened and reduced to about 3 cups, stirring occasionally. Stir in lemon peel and lemon verbena.

2 Ladle hot compote into hot, sterilized half-pint canning jars, leaving a ¼-inch headspace. Wipe jar rims; adjust lids.

3 Process filled jars in a boiling-water canner for 15 minutes (start timing when water returns to boiling). Remove jars from canner; cool on a wire rack. **Makes 3 half-pints.**

PER TABLESPOON: 56 cal., 0 g fat, 0 mg chol., 0 mg sodium, 14 g carbo., 0 g fiber, 0 g pro.

TEST KITCHEN *tip*

Delicate herbs such as tarragon, mint, and basil reach their peaks in the summer months. Rosemary, lavender, lemon verbena, thyme, and other hardier herbs hit their peaks in the fall.

Can It!

Geranium-Apple Jelly

The flavor of this jelly depends on which kind of scented geranium you choose. Scents of the plants include lemon, clove, ginger, and rose, just to name a few. For a simple but tasty dessert, dress up panna cotta ("cooked cream") with a dollop or two of the jelly.

PREP: 1 hour 15 minutes **COOK:** 15 minutes **STAND:** 2 hours **PROCESS:** 5 minutes

5   pounds cooking apples
    (such as Braeburn, Granny
    Smith, or Rome Beauty)
5   cups water
1   1.75-ounce package regular
    powdered fruit pectin
9   cups sugar
6   sprigs scented edible geranium

1 Remove and discard apple stems and blossom ends. Cut apples into small pieces (do not peel or core). Place apple pieces in an 8-quart heavy pot; add the water. Bring to boiling; reduce heat. Simmer, covered, for 10 minutes. Using a potato masher or back of a large spoon, crush cooked apples. Simmer, covered, for 5 minutes more, stirring occasionally. Line an extra-large strainer with 100%-cotton cheesecloth; place over an extra-large bowl. Pour apple mixture into strainer. Strain until dripping stops (about 2 hours). Press apple mixture gently with back of a spoon. Measure 7 cups juice;* return juice to the pot.

2 Stir pectin into apple juice in pot. Bring mixture to a full rolling boil. Stir in sugar. Return to full rolling boil. Boil hard for 1 minute. Gently stir the geranium sprigs through the liquid for about 30 seconds. Press the sprigs against the side of the pot to release all of their flavor. Remove sprigs from the juice mixture.

3 Ladle hot jelly into hot, sterilized half-pint canning jars, leaving a ¼-inch headspace. Wipe jar rims; adjust lids.

4 Process filled jars in a boiling-water canner for 5 minutes (start timing when water returns to boiling). Remove jars from canner; cool on wire racks. **Makes 10 half-pints.**

PER TABLESPOON: 52 cal., 0 g fat, 0 mg chol., 1 mg sodium, 14 g carbo., 0 g fiber, 0 g pro.

*TEST KITCHEN TIP: If you don't have 7 cups apple juice, add enough bottled apple juice to equal 7 cups total liquid. Do not attempt to make this jelly with all bottled apple juice; it will not set properly.

Rosemary-Lime Honeydew Jam

Honeydew is a very sweet melon—the addition of lime juice and rosemary balances its sweetness with a bit of acidity and astringency.

PREP: 35 minutes   **PROCESS:** 10 minutes

6   cups cubed, seeded, and peeled firm honeydew melon
½   cup lime juice
5½ cups sugar
½   teaspoon butter
1   6-ounce package liquid fruit pectin (2 foil pouches)
2   tablespoons finely snipped fresh rosemary

1 Place cubed melon in a food processor, half at a time, and process until mixture is smooth. Place pureed melon in a sieve and allow any excess liquid to drain from the crushed melon. Discard any liquid.

2 In a 6- to 8-quart heavy pot combine the crushed melon, lime juice, sugar, and butter. Bring to a boil over medium heat, stirring constantly until sugar dissolves; reduce heat to low. Simmer gently, uncovered, for 2 minutes, stirring frequently.

3 Increase heat to medium-high and bring to a full rolling boil, stirring constantly. Quickly stir in pectin; return to a full roilng boil; boil for 1 minute, stirring constantly. Remove from heat. If necessary, quickly skim off foam with a metal spoon. Stir in rosemary.

4 Ladle hot jam into hot, sterilized half-pint canning jars, leaving a ¼-inch headspace. Wipe jar rims; adjust lids.

5 Process filled jars in a boiling-water canner for 10 minutes (start timing when water returns to boiling). Remove jars; cool on wire racks. To distribute herbs, cool about 20 minutes, then gently turn and tilt jars without inverting them. Repeat as needed. **Makes about 6 half pints.**

PER TABLESPOON: 49 cal., 0 g fat, 0 mg chol., 2 mg sodium, 13 g carbo., 0 g fiber, 0 g protein.

TEST KITCHEN
tip

Choose melons that are just ripe; avoid overripe melons, which will cause the jam to be too sweet and may prevent it from setting up properly.

Homemade Pesto

For handy 2-tablespoon portions, store the pesto in an ice cube tray. Place 2 tablespoons of pesto in each slot of a standard ice cube tray; cover tightly with foil. Freeze for up to 3 months.

START TO FINISH: 15 minutes

3	cups firmly packed fresh basil leaves (3 ounces)
⅔	cup pine nuts and/or walnuts
⅔	cup grated Parmesan or Romano cheese
½	cup olive oil
4	cloves garlic, quartered
½	teaspoon salt
¼	teaspoon black pepper

1 In a food processor or blender, combine basil, nuts, cheese, olive oil, garlic, salt, and pepper. Cover and process or blend until nearly smooth, stopping to scrape the sides as necessary.

2 Ladle pesto into a hot, sterilized half-pint jar, leaving a ½-inch headspace. Seal and label. (Place any remaining pesto in an airtight storage container.) Store in the refrigerator for up to 2 days. To freeze, transfer to a freezer-safe container. Seal and label. Freeze for up to 3 months. **Makes 1¼ cups.**

PER 2 TABLESPOONS: 185 cal., 19 g fat (3 g sat. fat), 5 mg chol., 199 mg sodium, 2 g carbo., 1 g fiber, 4 g pro.

LEMON-HAZELNUT PESTO: Prepare as directed, except substitute hazelnuts for the pine nuts, use ⅔ cup hazelnut oil in place of the olive oil, and stir 1 tablespoon finely shredded lemon peel into pureed pesto.

SUN-DRIED TOMATO PESTO: Prepare as directed, except substitute 8.5 ounces (1 jar) dried tomatoes in oil for the olive oil and substitute finely shredded Asiago cheese for the Parmesan cheese.

CHAPTER 12

From the Vine

Vine-ripened treasures—pumpkins, squash, cucumbers, and watermelons—scrumptiously transform into magnificent jarred goodness with the utmost of ease.

Best-Ever Dill Pickles

If small pickling cucumbers are not available, cut field (regular garden) cucumbers into 4-inch spears—and be sure that any cucumber you pickle has not been waxed.

PREP: 30 minutes **PROCESS:** 10 minutes **STAND:** 1 week

3	to 3¼ pounds 4-inch pickling cucumbers* (about 36 small)
4	cups water
4	cups white vinegar
½	cup sugar
⅓	cup pickling salt
6	tablespoons dill seeds

1 Thoroughly scrub cucumbers with a soft vegetable brush in plenty of cold running water. Remove the stems and blossoms and slice off the blossom ends. Slice cucumbers into ¼- to ½-inch-thick slices.

2 In a 4- to 5-quart stainless-steel, enamel, or nonstick heavy pot combine the water, vinegar, sugar, and pickling salt. Bring mixture to boiling, stirring until sugar dissolves.

3 Pack cucumber slices loosely into hot, sterilized pint canning jars, leaving a ½-inch headspace. Add 1 tablespoon of the dill seeds to each jar. Pour hot vinegar mixture over cucumbers, maintaining the ½-inch headspace. Discard any remaining vinegar mixture. Wipe jar rims; adjust lids.

4 Process filled jars in a boiling-water canner for 10 minutes (start timing when water returns to boiling). Remove jars from canner; cool on wire racks. Allow to stand at room temperature for 1 week before serving. **Makes 6 pints.**

PER ¼ CUP: 25 cal., 0 g fat, 0 mg chol., 859 mg sodium, 5 g carbo., 0 g fiber, 0 g pro.

Crunchy Dill and Onion Chips: In a large bowl combine 12 cups sliced pickling cucumbers, 2 cups thinly sliced onions, and ⅓ cup pickling salt. Set a large stainless-steel or nonmetal colander in an extra-large stainless-steel or nonmetal bowl; in colander alternately layer cucumber mixture and crushed ice, ending with a layer of crushed ice. Weight down mixture with a heavy plate. Chill in the refrigerator overnight or for up to 24 hours. Remove any unmelted ice from cucumber mixture; discard any liquid in bowl. In a 4- to 5-quart stainless-steel, enamel, or nonstick heavy pot combine 4 cups water, 4 cups white vinegar, and ½ cup sugar. Bring mixture to boiling, stirring until sugar dissolves. Pack cucumbers and onions in jars as directed in Step 3 and continue as directed through Step 4. **Makes 5 pints.**

Bread and Butter Pickles

Try these sweet pickles on a hamburger or stir them, finely chopped, into mustardy potato salad.

PREP: 40 minutes   **CHILL:** 3 to 12 hours
PROCESS: 10 minutes

16	cups sliced small to medium pickling cucumbers (4 quarts)
8	medium white onions, sliced
⅓	cup pickling salt
3	cloves garlic, halved
	Crushed ice
4	cups sugar
3	cups cider vinegar
2	tablespoons mustard seeds
1½	teaspoons ground turmeric
1½	teaspoons celery seeds

1 In a 6- to 8-quart stainless-steel, enamel, or nonstick heavy pot combine cucumbers, onions, pickling salt, and garlic; top with 2 inches of crushed ice. Cover with lid and chill in the refrigerator for 3 to 12 hours.

2 Remove any remaining ice from pot; transfer cucumber mixture to a colander and drain. Remove garlic; discard.

3 In the same pot combine sugar, vinegar, mustard seeds, turmeric, and celery seeds. Bring to boiling, stirring until sugar dissolves. Add cucumber mixture. Return to boiling, then remove from heat.

4 Pack hot cucumber mixture and liquid into hot, sterilized pint canning jars, leaving a ½-inch headspace. Wipe jar rims; adjust lids.

5 Process filled jars in a boiling-water canner for 10 minutes (start timing when water returns to boiling). Remove jars from canner; cool on wire racks. **Makes 7 pints.**

PER ¼ CUP: 33 cal., 0 g fat, 0 mg chol., 266 mg sodium, 9 g carbo., 0 g fiber, 0 g pro.

Sweet Pickle Relish

Knock the next hot dog or bratwurst you grill out of the park with this fresh homemade relish.

PREP: 30 minutes   **STAND:** 2 hours   **COOK:** 10 minutes
PROCESS: 10 minutes

6	cups seeded and finely chopped pickling cucumbers (6 medium)
3	cups finely chopped onions (6 medium)
3	cups seeded and finely chopped green and/or red sweet peppers (3 large)
¼	cup pickling salt
	Cold water
3	cups sugar
2	cups cider vinegar
1	tablespoon mustard seeds
2	teaspoons celery seeds
½	teaspoon ground turmeric

1 In an extra-large nonmetal bowl combine cucumbers, onions, and sweet peppers. Sprinkle with salt; toss to coat. Add cold water to cover vegetables. Cover; allow to stand at room temperature for 2 hours.

2 Transfer vegetable mixture to a colander set in sink. Rinse with cold water; drain.

3 In an 8-quart stainless-steel, enamel, or nonstick heavy pot combine sugar, vinegar, mustard seeds, celery seeds, and turmeric. Bring to boiling, stirring until sugar dissolves. Add drained vegetable mixture. Return to boiling; reduce heat. Simmer, uncovered, for about 10 minutes or until most of the excess liquid has evaporated, stirring occasionally.

4 Ladle hot relish into hot, sterilized half-pint canning jars, leaving a ½-inch headspace. Wipe jar rims; adjust lids.

5 Process filled jars in a boiling-water canner for 10 minutes (start timing when water returns to boiling). Remove jars from canner; cool on wire racks. **Makes 7 half-pints.**

PER TABLESPOON: 22 cal., 0 g fat, 0 mg chol., 218 mg sodium, 5 g carbo., 0 g fiber, 0 g pro.

Bread and Butter Zucchini Pickles

These yummy little morsels add the perfect kick of sweetness to pulled pork sandwiches.

PREP: 55 minutes   **STAND:** 2 hours   **COOK:** 5 minutes   **PROCESS:** 10 minutes

3½	pounds medium zucchini
1	cup thinly sliced, halved onion (1 large)
3	tablespoons pickling salt
	Crushed ice
2	cups cider vinegar
1½	cups sugar
1	tablespoon mustard seeds
1	teaspoon celery seeds
½	teaspoon whole black peppercorns
½	teaspoon ground turmeric

1. Wash zucchini. Slice off the stem and blossom ends. Cut zucchini crosswise into ¼-inch-thick slices. Measure 12 cups zucchini slices.

2. In an extra-large nonmetal bowl combine the 12 cups zucchini and the 1 cup onion slices. Sprinkle with salt; toss gently to coat. Top with 2 inches of crushed ice. Weight down mixture with a heavy plate. Allow to stand at room temperature for 2 hours.

3. Remove any remaining ice in zucchini mixture. Transfer mixture to a colander set in sink; drain.

4. In a 5- to 6-quart stainless-steel, enamel, or nonstick heavy pot combine vinegar, sugar, mustard seeds, celery seeds, peppercorns, and turmeric. Bring to boiling, stirring until sugar dissolves. Add zucchini mixture. Return to boiling, stirring frequently; reduce heat. Simmer, uncovered, for 5 minutes.

5. Ladle hot mixture into hot, sterilized pint canning jars, leaving a ½-inch headspace. Wipe jar rims; adjust lids.

6. Process filled jars in a boiling-water canner for 10 minutes (start timing when water returns to boiling). Remove jars from canner; cool on wire racks. **Makes 5 pints.**

PER ¼ CUP: 11 cal., 0 g fat, 0 mg chol., 428 mg sodium, 9 g carbo., 1 g fiber, 1 g pro.

Hot and Spicy Zucchini Pickles

These zesty spears are great on their own but even better nestled in a bun next to a beer brat.

PREP: 1 hour   **STAND:** 3 hours   **PROCESS:** 10 minutes

4	pounds medium zucchini
4	cups ice cubes
¼	cup pickling salt
4	cups white vinegar
1⅔	cups water
1½	cups sugar
1	to 1½ teaspoons crushed red pepper
6	small fresh red serrano or Thai chile peppers (see tip, page 57)
6	small fresh green serrano or jalapeño chile peppers (see tip, page 57)
6	bay leaves
6	teaspoons whole black peppercorns
3	teaspoons mustard seeds

1 Wash zucchini. Slice off the stem and blossom ends. Cut zucchini into 3- to 4-inch-long spears (about ¾ inch thick; you should have about 16 cups zucchini spears).

2 In an extra-large nonmetal bowl layer one-third of the zucchini, one-third of the ice cubes, and one-third of the salt. Repeat layers twice. Weight down mixture with a heavy plate. Allow to stand at room temperature for 3 hours.

3 Remove any remaining ice from zucchini mixture; transfer zucchini mixture to a colander and drain.

4 In a 3-quart stainless-steel, enamel, or nonstick heavy pot combine vinegar, the water, sugar, and crushed red pepper. Bring to boiling over medium heat, stirring until sugar dissolves. Boil for 1 minute. Reduce heat to low to keep warm.

5 Pack zucchini into hot, sterilized pint canning jars. To each jar add 1 of the red chile peppers, 1 of the green chile peppers, 1 of the bay leaves, 1 teaspoon of the black peppercorns, and ½ teaspoon of the mustard seeds. Pour hot liquid into each jar to cover zucchini, leaving a ½-inch headspace. Remove any air bubbles in jars. If necessary, add more of the hot liquid. Wipe jar rims; adjust lids.

6 Process filled jars in a boiling-water canner for 10 minutes (start timing when water returns to boiling). Remove jars from canner; cool on wire racks. **Makes 6 pints.**

PER ¼ CUP: 38 cal., 0 g fat, 0 mg chol., 125 mg sodium, 8 g carbo., 1 g fiber, 1 g pro.

Zucchini and Sweet Pepper Refrigerator Pickles

Sweet, tart, and savory all at once, these easy-to-make pickles delightfully complement everything from hamburgers and hot dogs to fish sandwiches.

PREP: 45 minutes   **STAND:** 3 hours   **COOL:** 30 minutes   **CHILL:** 1 to 2 days

6   cups thinly sliced zucchini
3   cups thinly sliced green and/
    or red sweet peppers
1   cup thinly sliced onion (1 large)
1   tablespoon kosher salt
3   cups sugar
3   cups cider vinegar
3   cups water

1 In an extra-large nonmetal bowl combine zucchini, sweet peppers, and onion. Sprinkle mixture with salt; toss gently to coat. Add enough cold water to cover vegetables. Cover and allow to stand at room temperature for 3 hours.

2 Transfer vegetable mixture to a colander set in sink. Rinse with cold water; drain.

3 In a large stainless-steel, enamel, or nonstick heavy saucepan combine sugar, vinegar, and water. Bring to boiling, stirring until sugar dissolves. Remove from heat.

4 Pack vegetables into sterilized pint canning jars or other jars. Pour hot vinegar mixture over vegetables, making sure to cover vegetables. Cool for 30 minutes. Seal and label.

5 Chill for 1 to 2 days before serving. Store in the refrigerator for up to 1 month. **Makes about 5 pints.**

PER ¼ CUP: 27 cal., 0 g fat, 0 mg chol., 39 mg sodium, 7 g carbo., 0 g fiber, 0 g pro.

TEST KITCHEN tip

Look for firm, crisp zucchini that have shiny, vibrant green skin without cuts or soft spots. They should have moist stem ends, which indicate freshness. For the sweetest flavor and most tender texture, select small to medium zucchini no more than 8 inches long and 2½ inches around. Large zucchini tend to have too-thick skin and often become mushy when pickled.

Watermelon
Pickles

Watermelon Pickles

If you love salty-sweet flavor pairings, wrap a paper-thin slice of prosciutto around a chunk of pickled melon. Or for a healthful breakfast, dip bare pickled melon chunks in Greek yogurt.

PREP: 1 hour **STAND:** overnight **COOK:** 55 minutes **PROCESS:** 10 minutes

1	**10-pound watermelon**
6	**cups water**
⅓	**cup pickling salt**
3½	**cups sugar**
1½	**cups white vinegar**
1½	**cups water**
15	**inches stick cinnamon, broken**
2	**teaspoons whole cloves**

1 Cut rind from watermelon (you should have about 4½ pounds rind). Trim off the pink flesh and the green and pale green outer portions of the watermelon rind; discard those portions. Cut the rind into 1-inch squares or other 1-inch shapes. Measure 9 cups rind.

2 Place the 9 cups rind in a large nonmetal bowl. In another large bowl combine the 6 cups water and the pickling salt; pour over rind (add more water, if necessary, to cover rind). Cover bowl and allow to stand at room temperature overnight.

3 Pour the rind mixture into a colander set in sink. Rinse mixture under cold water; drain well. Transfer rind to a 4-quart heavy pot. Add enough cold water to cover rind. Bring to boiling; reduce heat. Simmer, covered, for 20 to 25 minutes or until rind is tender; drain.

4 Meanwhile, for syrup, in a 6- to 8-quart stainless-steel, enamel, or nonstick heavy pot combine sugar, vinegar, the 1½ cups water, the stick cinnamon, and cloves. Bring to boiling, stirring until sugar dissolves; reduce heat. Simmer, uncovered, for 10 minutes. Strain mixture through a sieve, reserving liquids. Discard solids and return liquids to same pot.

5 Add watermelon rind to syrup in pot. Bring to boiling; reduce heat. Simmer, covered, for 25 to 30 minutes or until rind is translucent.

6 Pack hot rind and syrup into hot, sterilized half-pint canning jars, leaving a ½-inch headspace. Wipe jar rims; adjust lids.

7 Process filled jars in a boiling-water canner for 10 minutes (start timing when water returns to boiling). Remove jars from canner; cool on wire racks. **Makes 6 half-pints.**

PER ¼ CUP: 117 cal., 0 g fat, 0 mg chol., 1,288 mg sodium, 30 g carbo., 0 g fiber, 0 g pro.

Spicy-Sweet Pickled Butternut Squash

Chop up a few of these sweet but savory pickled squash chunks and add them to a brown rice or wild rice pilaf. The nuttiness of the rice gets a tangy boost from the pickles.

PREP: 1 hour   **COOK:** 10 minutes   **STAND:** 3 to 4 hours + 3 weeks   **PROCESS:** 10 minutes

3	pounds butternut squash, peeled, seeded, and cut into ¾-inch cubes
2	tablespoons kosher salt
8	sprigs fresh oregano
2½	cups white wine vinegar
1	cup honey
2	teaspoons fennel seeds
1	teaspoon crushed red pepper
8	black peppercorns
3	cloves garlic, coarsely chopped
1	bay leaf

1. In a large bowl combine squash and salt; toss to coat. Let stand at room temperature for 3 to 4 hours. Transfer squash to a colander set in sink. Rinse with cold water; drain.

2. Pack the squash cubes and oregano sprigs into hot, sterilized pint canning jars, leaving a ½-inch headspace.

3. In a large stainless-steel, enamel, or nonstick heavy pot combine vinegar, honey, fennel seeds, crushed red pepper, peppercorns, garlic, and bay leaf. Bring to boiling over medium-high heat, stirring until honey dissolves; reduce heat to low. Simmer, covered, for 10 minutes. Remove from heat. Remove and discard bay leaf.

4. Ladle the hot vinegar mixture over the squash, maintaining the ½-inch headspace. Evenly distribute whole spices among the jars. Wipe jar rims; adjust lids.

5. Process filled jars in a boiling-water canner for 10 minutes (start timing when water returns to boiling). Remove jars from canner; cool on wire racks. Allow to stand at room temperature for 3 weeks before serving. **Makes 4 pints.**

PER ¼ CUP: 56 cal., 0 g fat, 0 mg chol., 94 mg sodium, 13 g carbo., 1 g fiber, 0 g pro.

TEST KITCHEN tip

To peel a butternut squash, cut off both ends using a large chef's knife. Cut the squash in half lengthwise; scrape out the seeds and fibrous strings from each half. Hold a squash half at an angle on your cutting board and use a sturdy vegetable peeler to peel down its length.

Spiced Pumpkin Butter

Jars of this sweetly spiced, maple syrup-infused fruit butter make a lovely hostess gift for a fall dinner party or holiday celebration. (Or keep it for yourself and try it on buckwheat pancakes.)

PREP: 15 minutes   **COOK:** 25 minutes   **COOL:** 30 minutes

3½   cups Pumpkin Puree or
      two 15-ounce cans pumpkin
1¼   cups pure maple syrup
½   cup apple juice
2   tablespoons lemon juice
1   teaspoon ground ginger
½   teaspoon ground cinnamon
½   teaspoon ground nutmeg
¼   teaspoon salt

1 In a 5-quart heavy pot combine pumpkin, maple syrup, apple juice, lemon juice, ginger, cinnamon, nutmeg, and salt. Bring to boiling; reduce heat. Simmer, uncovered, about 25 minutes or until thickened, stirring often. (If mixture spatters, reduce heat more.)

2 Ladle hot pumpkin butter into hot, sterilized half-pint canning jars, leaving a ½-inch headspace. Cool for 30 minutes. Seal and label.

3 Store in the refrigerator for up to 1 week or transfer to freezer containers, leaving ½-inch headspace, and freeze for up to 6 months. **Makes about 4 half-pints.**

Pumpkin Puree: Preheat oven to 375°F. Scrub two 2½- to 3-pound pie pumpkins thoroughly. Cut pumpkins into 5-inch-square pieces, discarding stems. Remove seeds and fibrous strings. Arrange pumpkin pieces in a single layer, skin sides up, in a foil-lined shallow baking pan. Roast, covered, for 1 to 1½ hours or until tender. When cool enough to handle, scoop pulp from rind. Place pulp, in batches if necessary, in a blender or food processor. Cover and blend or process until smooth. Place puree in a fine-mesh sieve lined with a double thickness of 100%-cotton cheesecloth. Let stand for 1 hour to drain. Press lightly to remove any additional liquid; discard liquid.

PER 2 TABLESPOONS: 35 cal., 0 g fat, 0 mg chol., 17 mg sodium, 9 g carbo., 0 g fiber, 0 g pro.

CHAPTER 13

Meant for Giving

Few gifts secure smiles like gleaming jars filled with treasures created using your own time and talent. These handcrafted treats are perfect for any gift-giving occasion.

Vanilla Bean Liqueur

Drink this straight up in cordial glasses—or stir a bit into a cup of coffee and top with whipped cream.

PREP: 10 minutes   **STAND:** 1 month

2   **cups vodka**
1   **cup sugar**
3   **vanilla beans, split in half crosswise and lengthwise**
     Vanilla beans (optional)

1 In a sterilized quart screw-top jar combine vodka, sugar, and the split vanilla beans. Cover tightly and shake jar until sugar dissolves.

2 Allow mixture to stand (steep) in a cool, dark place for 1 month. Remove vanilla beans; discard.

3 Transfer liqueur to clean, decorative bottles with tight-fitting lids. If desired, add a vanilla bean to each bottle for garnish. Seal and label. Store at room temperature. **Makes 2½ cups.**

PER 2 TABLESPOONS: 92 cal., 0 g fat, 0 mg chol., 0 mg sodium, 10 g carbo., 0 g fiber, 0 g pro.

Limoncello

In Italy, this aromatic lemon liqueur is enjoyed as a digestif after dinner.

PREP: 25 minutes   **STAND:** 10 days
COOL: 30 minutes   **CHILL:** overnight

10	large lemons
1	750-milliliter bottle vodka
3	cups sugar
2½	cups water

1 Thoroughly scrub lemons with a vegetable brush. Using a vegetable peeler, remove the yellow portion of the peel in narrow strips; measure 2 cups lemon peel. (If desired, juice lemons and reserve juice for another use.)

2 In a sterilized 2-quart glass jar combine the 2 cups lemon peel and vodka. Cover jar with a tight-fitting lid. Allow to stand (steep) in a cool, dry place for 10 days, gently swirling the mixture in the jar each day.

3 Strain mixture through a fine-mesh sieve set in a large bowl; discard lemon peel. Return the lemon-infused vodka to the jar.

4 For syrup, in a medium saucepan combine sugar and the water. Bring to boiling, stirring until sugar dissolves. Remove from heat; cool for 30 minutes.

5 Pour cooled syrup into the lemon-infused vodka; stir to combine. Cover and chill overnight. Transfer limoncello to sterilized half-pint jars or bottles. Seal and label. Store for up to 1 month in the refrigerator. **Makes about 7 half-pints.**

PER 2 TABLESPOONS: 72 cal., 0 g fat, 0 mg chol., 1 mg sodium, 11 g carbo., 0 g fiber, 0 g pro.

Cranberry and Jalapeño Pepper Jelly

Regulate the hotness of the jelly by using two, three, or four jalapeños. Remove and discard seeds for a more mild result.

PREP: 50 minutes **COOK:** 11 minutes **PROCESS:** 5 minutes

1½ cups cranberry juice (not low-calorie)
1 cup vinegar
2 to 4 medium fresh jalapeño chile peppers, halved and, if desired, seeded (see tip, page 57)
5 cups sugar
½ of a 6-ounce package (1 foil pouch) liquid fruit pectin
5 small fresh red serrano or Thai chile peppers (see tip, page 57)

1 In a medium stainless-steel, enamel, or nonstick heavy saucepan combine cranberry juice, vinegar, and jalapeño peppers. Bring to boiling; reduce heat. Simmer, covered, for 10 minutes. Strain mixture through a fine-mesh sieve set in a medium bowl, pressing with the back of a spoon to remove all the liquid; discard pulp. Measure 2 cups liquid.

2 In a 5- to 6-quart stainless-steel, enamel, or nonstick heavy pot combine the 2 cups liquid and the sugar. Bring to a full rolling boil, stirring constantly until sugar dissolves. Stir in pectin and serrano peppers. Return to a full rolling boil, stirring constantly. Boil hard for 1 minute, stirring constantly. Remove from heat. Skim off foam with a metal spoon.

3 Ladle hot jelly into hot, sterilized half-pint canning jars, leaving a ¼-inch headspace. Add a serrano pepper to each jar. Wipe jar rims; adjust lids.

4 Process filled jars in a boiling-water canner for 5 minutes (start timing when water returns to boiling). Remove jars from canner; cool on wire racks. **Makes 5 half-pints.**

PER TABLESPOON: 57 cal., 0 g fat, 0 mg chol., 0 mg sodium, 15 g carbo., 0 g fiber, 0 g pro.

Pomegranate Jelly

Pomegranate Jelly

This festive jelly couldn't be any easier to make—there's no cutting, chopping, or cleaning of fruit. Just combine ingredients, cook, and process.

PREP: 25 minutes   **PROCESS:** 5 minutes

4	cups pomegranate juice
¼	cup lemon juice
1	1.75-ounce package regular powdered fruit pectin
4½	cups sugar

1 In a 6- to 8-quart heavy pot combine pomegranate juice and lemon juice. Sprinkle juices with pectin. Let stand at room temperature for 1 to 2 minutes; stir to dissolve pectin. Bring to a full rolling boil, stirring frequently. Stir in sugar. Return to a full rolling boil, stirring constantly. Boil hard for 1 minute, stirring constantly. Remove from heat. Quickly skim off foam with a metal spoon.

2 Ladle hot jelly into hot, sterilized half-pint canning jars, leaving a ¼-inch headspace. Wipe jar rims; adjust lids.

3 Process filled jars in a boiling-water canner for 5 minutes (start timing when water returns to boiling). Remove jars from canner; cool on wire racks. Let stand at room temperature until jelly sets. **Makes 5 half-pints.**

PER TABLESPOON: 68 cal., 0 g fat, 0 mg chol., 2 mg sodium, 18 g carbo., 0 g fiber, 0 g pro.

TEST KITCHEN *tip*

Attach a small spreader or jelly spoon to the jar with a piece of yarn. Add a tag and your homemade gift is ready to give.

Ginger Chutney

The perfect accompaniment to a holiday ham, this chunky pear, sweet pepper, and onion chutney is flavored with ginger, lemon, lime, cinnamon, and cayenne.

PREP: 30 minutes **COOK:** 35 minutes **PROCESS:** 10 minutes

2 cups packed brown sugar
¾ cup vinegar
½ cup water
½ teaspoon salt
¼ teaspoon ground cinnamon
¼ teaspoon cayenne pepper
1 large lemon
1 large lime
3 cups coarsely chopped, peeled Anjou pears (about 1 pound)
1 cup chopped green sweet pepper (1 large)
1 cup chopped red sweet pepper (1 large)
1 cup chopped onion (1 large)
1 cup golden raisins
1 tablespoon finely chopped crystallized ginger

1 In a 4- to 5-quart stainless-steel, enamel, or nonstick heavy pot stir together brown sugar, vinegar, the water, salt, cinnamon, and cayenne pepper. Bring to boiling; reduce heat. Simmer, uncovered, for 10 minutes, stirring occasionally. Meanwhile, finely shred peel from lemon and lime (you should have about 2 tablespoons peel total); squeeze juice from lemon and lime (you should have about ⅓ cup juice total).

2 Add peels, juices, pears, sweet peppers, onion, raisins, and crystallized ginger to hot mixture in pot. Return to boiling; reduce heat to medium-low. Simmer, uncovered, for about 25 minutes or until mixture is thick, stirring occasionally (you should have about 3¾ cups).

3 Ladle hot chutney into hot, sterilized half-pint canning jars, leaving a ¼-inch headspace. Wipe jar rims; adjust lids.

4 Process filled jars in a boiling-water canner for 10 minutes (start timing when water returns to boiling). Remove jars from canner; cool on wire racks. **Makes 4 half-pints.**

PER 2 TABLESPOONS: 83 cal., 0 g fat, 0 mg chol., 43 mg sodium, 21 g carbo., 1 g fiber, 0 g pro.

TEST KITCHEN *tip*

Crystallized ginger adds a nice touch of heat to this exquisite chutney. Look for it in the baking aisle of your supermarket.

Honey-
chianti
jelly

Honey-Chianti Jelly

You can really use any kind of dry red wine you like to drink to make this honeyed jelly. It's delicious served as an accompaniment to roasted beef tenderloin.

PREP: 25 minutes   **PROCESS:** 5 minutes

1	**1.75-ounce package regular powdered fruit pectin**
2	**cups Chianti, Sangiovese, or other dry red wine**
3½	**cups honey**
¼	**teaspoon butter**

1 In a 4-quart heavy pot stir pectin into wine. Allow to stand at room temperature for 1 to 2 minutes, stirring until pectin dissolves. Bring to a full rolling boil, stirring constantly. Stir in honey. Return to boiling. Add butter; boil for 2 minutes more, stirring constantly. Remove from heat. Quickly skim off foam with a metal spoon.

2 Ladle hot jelly into hot, sterilized half-pint canning jars, leaving a ¼-inch headspace. Wipe jar rims; adjust lids.

3 Process filled jars in a boiling-water canner for 5 minutes (start timing when water returns to boiling). Remove jars from canner; cool on wire racks. **Makes about 6 half-pints.**

PER TABLESPOON: 45 cal., 0 g fat, 0 mg chol., 1 mg sodium, 11 g carbo., 0 g fiber, 0 g pro.

TEST KITCHEN *tip*

Place a paper cocktail napkin over the top of the sealed jar. Twist the lid down over the top of the napkin to create a ruffled look.

Peppery Peach Sauce

Be sure to give this sweet and spicy sauce a good stir before serving it with broiled, roasted, or grilled poultry, pork, or ham.

PREP: 30 minutes   **COOK:** 15 minutes   **PROCESS:** 15 minutes

4	pounds fresh peaches or three 16-ounce packages frozen unsweetened peach slices
2	cups sugar
1	5.5-ounce can peach or apricot nectar
¼	cup cider vinegar
1	tablespoon lemon juice
1	fresh red chile pepper or habanero chile pepper, seeded and very finely chopped (about 1 tablespoon) (see tip, page 57)
½	teaspoon salt
2	cloves garlic, minced
1½	cups fresh raspberries

1 Wash fresh peaches, if using. Peel and pit peaches. Place half of the fresh or frozen peaches in a food processor or blender. Cover and process or blend until peaches are very finely chopped. Transfer chopped peaches to a 6-quart pot. Repeat with remaining peaches. (You should have 5 cups pureed peaches.)

2 Add sugar, nectar, vinegar, lemon juice, chile pepper, salt, and garlic to pot. Bring to boiling; reduce heat. Simmer, uncovered, for 15 to 20 minutes or until desired consistency, stirring occasionally. Remove from heat. Stir in raspberries.

3 Ladle hot sauce into hot, sterilized half-pint canning jars, leaving a ¼-inch headspace. Remove air bubbles, wipe jar rims, and fasten lids. Process filled jars in a boiling-water canner for 15 minutes (start timing when water returns to boil). Remove jars from canner; cool on racks. Include serving directions with gift. **Makes 8 half-pints.**

PER ¼ CUP: 147 cal., 5 g fat (2 g sat. fat), 18 mg chol., 124 mg sodium, 24 g carbo., 1 g fiber, 3 g pro.

Maple Applesauce

For more flavor varieties of applesauce that you can package prettily and give away as gifts, see page 171.

PREP: 1 hour **COOK:** 25 minutes **PROCESS:** 15 minutes (pints) 20 minutes (quarts)

8   **pounds tart cooking apples (about 24 medium)**

2   **cups water**

10   **inches stick cinnamon (optional)**

¾   **to 1¼ cups pure maple syrup**

1 Core and quarter apples. In an 8- to 10-quart heavy pot combine apples, the water, and, if desired, stick cinnamon. Bring to boiling; reduce heat. Cover and simmer for 25 to 35 minutes or until apples are very tender, stirring often.

2 Remove and discard cinnamon if used. Press apples through a food mill or sieve. Return pulp to pot. Stir in enough of the maple syrup to sweeten as desired. If necessary, stir in an additional ½ to 1 cup water to make desired consistency. Bring to boiling, stirring constantly.

3 Ladle hot applesauce into hot, sterilized pint or quart canning jars, leaving a ½-inch headspace. Wipe jar rims and fasten lids. Process filled jars in a boiling-water canner for 15 minutes for pints or 20 minutes for quarts (start timing when water returns to boil). Remove jars from canner; cool on wire racks. **Makes 6 pints or 3 quarts.**

PER ½ CUP: 80 cal., 0 g fat, 0 mg chol., 1 mg sodium, 21 g carbo., 2 g fiber, 0 g pro.

TEST KITCHEN tip

To dress up your applesauce jars, cut the sleeve of an old sweater 2 inches longer than the height of the jar. Turn the sleeve inside out and stitch the cut end closed. Turn the sleeve right side out and slide the sleeve over the jar. Tape a gift tag to the jar so the tag hangs out over the sweater.

Old-Fashioned Grape Jelly

Grapes in this jelly should be at two stages of ripeness: Less-ripe grapes contribute more pectin, helping the jelly to set. More-ripe grapes lend a richer, fuller flavor.

PREP: 45 minutes **COOK:** 30 minutes **STAND:** 4 hours 30 minutes **CHILL:** 12 to 14 hours
PROCESS: 5 minutes

6	pounds Concord grapes (use about 4½ pounds fully ripe grapes and about 1½ pounds firm, slightly less-ripe grapes)
¾	cup water
3¾	cups sugar

1 Wash and stem grapes. In a 6- to 8-quart kettle or pot crush grapes with a potato masher. Add the water. Bring to boiling over high heat; reduce heat. Simmer, covered, about 10 minutes or until grapes are very soft.

2 Using a jelly bag or a colander lined with several layers of 100%-cotton cheesecloth, strain the mixture. (This will take about 4½ hours.) You should have about 7 cups of juice. Refrigerate the juice for 12 to 14 hours. Strain again through the clean jelly bag or cheesecloth, being careful to strain out sediment.

3 Place juice in the same kettle. Add sugar; stir to dissolve. Bring to a full rolling boil. Boil hard, uncovered, until syrup sheets off a metal spoon or reaches 220°F. This will take about 20 minutes. Remove from heat. Quickly skim off foam with a metal spoon.

4 Immediately ladle jelly into hot, sterilized half-pint canning jars, leaving a ¼-inch headspace. Wipe jar rims; adjust lids. Process filled jars in a boiling-water canner for 5 minutes (start timing when water returns to boil). Remove jars from canner; cool on wire racks.
Makes 5 half-pints.

PER TABLESPOON: 52 cal., 0 g fat, 0 g chol., 0 mg sodium, 14 g carbo., 1 g fiber, 0 g pro.

TROUBLESHOOTING

Most of the time, if you follow a recipe exactly and employ stringent standards of cleanliness, your canned goods will come out perfectly. However, sometimes something goes wrong—either because of human error or compromised ingredients. Here's a rundown of some common problems and their solutions.

PICKLES

PROBLEM	CAUSE	SOLUTION
Soft or slippery pickles.	Enzymes, which soften pickles, were not inactivated or the brine and heat didn't work in preserving the pickles properly.	Always cut off the blossom end of the cucumbers because enzymes are concentrated there. Make sure the brine is full strength (measure carefully) and use pure, refined, or pickling salt. Remove scum daily during a long brining process. Cover pickles completely with liquid during any fermentation times and when processing in jars. Process all pickles in boiling-water canner, not a pressure canner.
Pickles shrivel in the jar.	Cucumbers did not properly absorb brine.	Precisely measure salt, sugar, and vinegar and mix well before adding to cucumbers. Prick whole cucumbers before canning. Never use waxed cucumbers (you can tell by scraping your nail along the peel).
Pickles darken or discolor in the jar.	Minerals or metals reacted with the brine, or spices were too fine or left in.	Use soft water when making brine. Use nonmetallic, nonreactive pans, bowls, and utensils when making pickles. Use whole spices, rather than ground, and remove them as the recipe directs.
White sediment forms in the bottom of pickle jar.	Yeasts have developed on the surface and settled or additives in salt have settled. (If there is any sign of spoilage or an odd smell, discard.)	The yeasts are harmless, as is the sediment if the amount of sediment is small. Use canning or pickling salt, which is specially formulated to be free of additives that can cloud or mar brine.

CONDIMENTS

PROBLEM	CAUSE	SOLUTION
Foods become black, brown, or gray in the jar.	Natural substances in the foods may be reacting with metal kitchen tools or hard water.	Use soft water for canning foods. Use nonmetallic, nonreactive pans, bowls, and utensils. If there is any sign of spoilage or an odd or unpleasant odor, discard.
Jar seals properly after processing but comes unsealed during storage.	Food could be spoiling and gases expanding, or the lid wasn't put on properly, or too much air remained in the jar after processing. (Never use a jar that has come open, even if it looks and smells safe.)	Use a current, reliable recipe and process for the recommended period of time. Follow exactly the instructions on page 21 for putting on lids. Make sure you are precise in creating the headspace specified in the recipe. Always slide a nonmetallic thin spatula around the sides of the filled jar before putting on the lid to get out air bubbles.
Loss of liquid during processing.	Too much air was in the jar before processing or processing wasn't done correctly.	Add the correct amount of liquid, as directed, during raw-pack recipes and measure headspace carefully. Or use a hot-pack method recipe, which assures less air in the jar. Always slide a nonmetallic thin spatula around the sides of the filled jar before putting on the lid to get out air bubbles. Make sure boiling-water process jars are covered with 1 to 2 inches of water at all times during timing. Keep pressure consistent during pressure canning.

JAMS, JELLIES, AND PRESERVES

PROBLEM	CAUSE	SOLUTION
Contains crystals.	The amount of sugar or cooking time may have been off or the method was wrong.	Measure sugar and other ingredients precisely. Cook traditional jams the specified time. Cooking too little doesn't allow sugar to dissolve; cooking too long results in too much evaporation. If sugar crystals stick to side of the pan during cooking, carefully wipe them off before filling jars.
Too soft or runny.	Pectin, which interacts with natural and added sugar and acid, was not allowed to develop properly.	Measure sugar, pectin, and other ingredients precisely. Do not double recipes for jams and jellies. Fruit may have been overripe with too much natural sugar. If cooked, the preserves may not have been boiled long enough at a rolling boil.
Contains bubbles.	Spoilage or trapped air.	If bubbles are moving when the jar is still, the preserves have spoiled and should be discarded. If the bubbles are not moving when the jar is still, it was not ladled quickly enough into the jar. Also, pour jam on the rim of the ladle, rather than directly into the jar, to prevent bubbles.
Mold occurs during storage.	Too much headspace or improper processing.	Never use a wax seal with preserves. This outdated method encourages spoilage. Process in a boiling-water canner instead. Leave a ¼-inch headspace with preserves. Measure carefully. Process for the time specified in a current, reliable recipe.

FRUITS AND VEGETABLES

PROBLEM	CAUSE	SOLUTION
Fruit floats in the jar.	Fruit is lighter than the syrup or isn't packed in tightly.	Use firm, ripe fruit, which is heavier. Next time use a hot-pack method (see page 18), which makes fruit heavier as it absorbs more liquid. Use a light to medium syrup. Pack fruit as firmly as you can without crushing it.
Food at top of jar gets dark over time while in the jar.	The food came in contact with air.	Use a hot-pack method, which slightly breaks down food and ensures it will sink lower and pack better into the jar. Use a thin plastic spatula or other flexible, long tool around the sides when packing in food to remove air bubbles. Make sure food is completely covered with liquid when packing and always process for the recommended time in a current, reliable recipe.
Fruit gets darker after opening.	The food was not processed long enough or at a high enough temperature to inactivate enzymes.	Follow a current, reliable recipe. Start timing boiling-water canned goods only when water reaches a rolling boil, not before.
White sediment forms in the bottom of a jar of vegetables.	This could be simply starch from the food or minerals in the water used. However, if the liquid is murky or the food is soft, it could be bacterial spoilage. Do not eat.	There is no way to inactivate starches in foods. Mineral deposits from water can be avoided by using soft water. Bacterial spoilage occurs when food isn't processed correctly or long enough.
Apples, pears, and peaches take on a purple to red color.	A natural chemical change has occurred during the heating process.	None. The change is harmless.
Black spots form on the underside of the metal lid.	Natural compounds in some foods make a brown or black deposit on the inside of the lid.	None. The deposits are harmless as long as there is no gray (which indicates mold) and there is no unpleasant or odd smell.

INDEX

ALTITUDE ADJUSTMENT

Water boils at a higher temperature at higher altitudes, which means that when you are canning at higher elevations, you must process food longer to ensure that it is safe to eat when stored at room temperature.

What is the elevation where you live? You may be surprised at how high it is. Much of the flat Midwest, for example, is above 1,000 feet. Check your community's altitude online before you begin canning so you can adjust processing times appropriately according to the following guidelines.

BLANCHING: Add 1 minute if you live 5,000 feet or more above sea level.

BOILING-WATER CANNER: Call your county extension service for detailed instructions.

JELLIES AND JAMS: Add 1 minute of processing time for each additional 1,000 feet.

STERILIZING JARS: Boil jars an additional 1 minute for each additional 1,000 feet.

METRIC INFORMATION

PRODUCT DIFFERENCES

Most of the ingredients called for in the recipes in this book are available in most countries. However, some are known by different names. Here are some common American ingredients and their possible counterparts:

- Sugar (white) is granulated, fine granulated, or castor sugar.
- Green, red, or yellow sweet peppers are capsicums or bell peppers.
- Golden raisins are sultanas.

VOLUME AND WEIGHT

The United States traditionally uses cup measures for liquid and solid ingredients. The chart below shows the approximate imperial and metric equivalents. If you are accustomed to weighing solid ingredients, the following approximate equivalents will be helpful.

- Canadian and U.S. volume for a cup measure is 8 fluid ounces (237 ml), but the standard metric equivalent is 250 ml.
- 1 British imperial cup is 10 fluid ounces.
- In Australia, 1 tablespoon equals 20 ml, and there are 4 teaspoons in the Australian tablespoon.
- Spoon measures are used for smaller amounts of ingredients. Although the size of the tablespoon varies slightly in different countries, for practical purposes and for recipes in this book, a straight substitution is all that's necessary. Measurements made using cups or spoons always should be level unless stated otherwise.

COMMON WEIGHT RANGE REPLACEMENTS

Imperial / U.S.	Metric
¼ ounce	15 g
1 ounce	25 g or 30 g
4 ounces (¼ pound)	115 g or 125 g
8 ounces (½ pound)	225 g or 250 g
16 ounces (1 pound)	450 g or 500 g
1¼ pounds	625 g
1¼ pounds	750 g
2 pounds or 2¼ pounds	1,000 g or 1 Kg

OVEN TEMPERATURE EQUIVALENTS

Fahrenheit Setting	Celsius Setting	Gas Setting
300°F	150°C	Gas Mark 2 (very low)
325°F	160°C	Gas Mark 3 (low)
350°F	180°C	Gas Mark 4 (moderate)
375°F	190°C	Gas Mark 5 (moderate)
400°F	200°C	Gas Mark 6 (hot)
425°F	220°C	Gas Mark 7 (hot)
450°F	230°C	Gas Mark 8 (very hot)
475°F	240°C	Gas Mark 9 (very hot)
500°F	260°C	Gas Mark 10 (extremely hot)
Broil	Broil	Grill

*Electric and gas ovens may be calibrated using celsius. However, for an electric oven, increase celsius setting 10 to 20 degrees when cooking above 160°C. For convection or forced-air ovens (gas or electric), lower the temperature setting 25°F/10°C when cooking at all heat levels.

U.S. / STANDARD METRIC EQUIVALENTS

⅛ teaspoon = 0.5 ml	
¼ teaspoon = 1 ml	
½ teaspoon = 2 ml	
1 teaspoon = 5 ml	
1 tablespoon = 15 ml	
2 tablespoons = 25 ml	
¼ cup = 2 fluid ounces = 50 ml	
⅓ cup = 3 fluid ounces = 75 ml	
½ cup = 4 fluid ounces = 125 ml	
⅔ cup = 5 fluid ounces = 150 ml	
¾ cup = 6 fluid ounces = 175 ml	
1 cup = 8 fluid ounces = 250 ml	
2 cups = 1 pint = 500 ml	
1 quart = 1 litre	